CW00428039

Warwickshire
MURDERS

Kevin Turton

SUTTON PUBLISHING

First published in the United Kingdom in 2007 by
Sutton Publishing Limited · Phoenix Mill
Thrupp · Stroud · Gloucestershire · GL5 2BU

Copyright © Kevin Turton, 2007

All rights reserved. No part of this publication may be reproduced, stored in a
retrieval system, or transmitted, in any form or by any means, electronic,
mechanical, photocopying, recording or otherwise, without the prior permission of
the publisher and copyright holder.

Kevin Turton has asserted the moral right to be identified as the author of this work.

British Library Cataloguing in Publication Data
A catalogue record for this book is available from the British Library.

ISBN 978-0-7509-4242-3

Typeset in 10.5/13.5pt Sabon.
Typesetting and origination by
Sutton Publishing Limited.
Printed and bound in England.

CONTENTS

INTRODUCTION & ACKNOWLEDGEMENTS

Murder is a heinous crime. It strips individuals of both their privacy and their dignity. Lives are often laid bare in open court and penalties inflicted on the perpetrators of such crimes are often considered by the public at large as being derisory. This perception, of course, is borne out by the numerous bar-room conversations up and down the country and the often sensationalised reporting by numerous newspapers. We all, at times, believe that courts are far too lenient and penalties not severe enough when it comes to murder. But unfortunately for most there is no direct access to the facts of each individual case because we cannot all attend court. This in turn means our judgements are flawed. We base our opinions on the columns of newsprint we read or the few minutes given over to cases by the television news channels. We are not able to be objective simply because we are not in possession of the full facts.

There are, as we all know, two sides to any argument and it follows there are also two sides to any murder case. Yet when it comes to the most serious of crimes, that of taking a life, we tend not to hear or read of the true and pertinent facts: those facts that influence juries and in turn dictate the severity of the sentences handed down by judges. Instead we are often swept along by a tide of journalistic hysteria that in turn clouds our own usually well-balanced views of life, almost forcing us to share, and agree, with the words on the page. But it has not always been like this.

When murder was a capital offence, which means the whole of history and the first sixty-odd years of the twentieth century, reporting bias was unheard of. Sensational headlines were not the common lot of newspapers and people were given greater access to accurate information through their local and national press. At a time when those that did kill stood to lose their lives on the scaffold, perhaps this stark, if brutal, reality ensured less bias and demanded a more sober and reflective level of reporting, though I doubt it.

The world, if we need reminding, was a very different place throughout this period. Certainly up to the turn of the nineteenth century life was cheap and severe penalties awaited those that transgressed against society's laws. Murder was only one of a range of offences that demanded the ultimate sacrifice and all were well reported by the press corps. Yet murder was still the crime that ate up more column inches than anything else the courts ever dealt with. There was a very real appetite among the reading public throughout this period for stories that reflected the darker side of life. As education spread across the country and more and more people came out of schools with the necessary reading skills to increase newspaper sales, so these new-found subscribers to the printed page began to make demands. Education had created an environment in which knowledge, not only of world events but also of local events, was gaining ever-increasing importance. As the population at large developed its reading skills, therefore, so it began to demand of those who produced the newsprint a greater level of accuracy. This then led to almost verbatim reporting of murder trials at a local level. With no other distractions, no television and no radio (limited until at least the 1940s), this type of narrative began to capture an audience hitherto unheard of and, for once, an audience whose views and opinions were not formed by headlines emblazoned across the front page. It was this public that first saw details of the crimes I have chosen to include here.

In *Warwickshire Murders* I have deliberately only chosen those cases that dominated the county and only cases where a guilty verdict would send the killer to the scaffold. It has been a long and extremely interesting journey. En route I have met, figuratively speaking, with a number of characters that certainly lived out their time on the darker side of life. Many were extremely unpleasant and deserving of nothing but contempt, but there are others for whom I can only feel deep sympathy. All played out their lives, albeit for a short period, in the public arena of a courtroom and all have a story to tell. I have endeavoured, therefore, to breathe life back into them so that they may tell their story a second time. I hope you are moved by much of what you read but above all else I hope you experience a similar journey.

I should like to thank the library staff at Warwick, Coventry and Stratford-upon-Avon, all of whom helped me source relevant material for the book. Likewise Warwickshire Records Office, and a long list of anonymous newspaper reporters whose attention to detail has proved inestimable. My thanks also go to authors past and present whose work has aided my own. They include *Perfect Murder* by Stephen Knight and Bernard Taylor; *Murder by Witchcraft* by Donald McCormick; *Warwickshire Tales of Mystery & Murder* by Betty Smith; *Midland Murders and Mysteries* by Barrie Roberts; *Terrible Murder of a Policeman* by Joseph Poland; *The Encyclopaedia of Executions* by John J. Eddleston; *Warwickshire Advertiser and Leamington Gazette*; *Coventry Evening Telegraph*; and *Cause of Death* by Keith D. Wilson. All pictures are from the author's collection unless otherwise stated. Every attempt has been made to trace and contact the original owners of any other images used in this book where relevant. If copyright has been inadvertently infringed it is unintentional.

1

A DEADLY SECRET

Mary Green, alias Polly Button, moved her family to the outskirts of Nuneaton at some point in 1828, taking a house at what was then known as Abbey End, a small terrace at the bottom of Abbey Street just outside the main town. Behind her lay two broken relationships and with her the product of those failed affairs in the shape of four children. Whether or not their by now absent fathers contributed to the family purse is not known, nor is Mary's occupation, though it is likely she had worked in the textile industry in one guise or another and quite possibly turned occasionally to prostitution. Money in the Green household, however, was always in short supply and Mary constantly sought a benefactor to ease her financial pressures. By the dawn of 1829 she had succeeded in finding a likely candidate in the form of near neighbour John Danks.

Danks was married but had no children and was no doubt an enthusiastic partner. The affair was hidden from prying eyes for much of that year, but by the autumn Mary had found herself pregnant for a fifth time. Unable to hide the relationship any longer their clandestine meetings were inevitably uncovered and Danks was forced to acknowledge both his involvement and his culpability. When

Mary gave birth to baby Jane in the early months of 1830 the notion of paternity seemed to sit well on his shoulders and he readily agreed to make regular weekly payments towards his daughter's upkeep. Perhaps the affair ought to have ended at that point. But it did not.

The view from Abbey End today looking towards Abbey Street. (Author's Collection)

Abbey Street today. In the nineteenth century this is where two-thirds of Nuneaton's population lived. The Burgage, which lies behind the buildings on the left, is built up now but was once open land owned and leased by the abbey. (Author's Collection)

Over the next eighteen months or so they continued to meet. How regularly those meetings took place or how important Danks was to Mary is unknown, but certainly by the winter of 1831 she was pregnant with her sixth child and the finger of guilt was again pointed in his direction. Unfortunately for Mary this was one baby John Danks was not prepared to allow into the world.

At the back of the terraced row where Mary lived lay open fields known locally as the Burgage (today Burgage Walk); a narrow track led from the back yards to a stile and, some way beyond, a gate. From its position straddling the track the gate probably marked a sort of boundary or marked the entrance to what was known as Astley's Hovel. This was simply a ramshackle, dilapidated, mean dwelling but a place where the couple often met. On 18 February 1832 at about 8 p.m., with Mary possibly some eight months pregnant and clearly showing, Danks decided they should meet for one last time. Not wanting to be seen at her door he hid in the yard and threw a handful of stones at her kitchen window to catch her attention, something he had done many times in the past. Mary, of course, knew the instant the stones hit the glass who had thrown them and had no hesitation in going out to meet him. Unfortunately for Danks the meeting in the yard was seen by Mary's eldest daughter, 18-year-old Elizabeth, who had gone out minutes earlier to meet her cousin. From their hidden vantage point in a nearby passageway they saw Danks emerge from the shadows and watched as the two talked. It was a cold night, and after a few minutes of conversation Mary ran back to the house to fetch a shawl and the two went off towards the Burgage.

At about seven the next morning a Nuneaton draper, Richard Beasley, who owned a field near to where Mary had last been seen heading, found her heavily bloodstained body. It lay face down in the centre of the narrow track some 15yds away from the hovel. She was clearly dead. As there was nothing he could do for Mary he sent his manservant off in search of the police and a surgeon and waited by the body. Police presence in the shape of constable to the parish, Joseph Haddon, was on the scene within the hour and here the parish was very lucky. Haddon was no average policeman. He took his role in the fledgling police force extremely seriously. Once Mary's body had been removed to her own home he closed off the area and began a thorough search of the ground around where she had been found. In modern-day parlance he did his utmost to secure the scene.

According to local surgeon, Dr Bond, Mary had been attacked with a knife; she had been battered on the left side of her head and her throat cut in three different places causing her to lose a great amount of blood. From her position on the track where she had been found, which was on the Abbey End side of the gate leading to the hovel, she had also survived the attack long enough to attempt to reach home. The evidence for this was borne out by the blood trail Constable Haddon discovered, which stretched from where her body lay back along the track, over the gate and into the hovel itself. Piecing all the evidence together he was able to show

The outer wall of Warwick prison today. All public executions took place on this street. (Author's Collection)

that Mary had been attacked inside the hovel, where she had sustained most of her injuries, and quite probably again by the gate. The comprehensive search he then carried out revealed a button torn off during the attack and two clear footprints in cow dung that covered much of the ground where the greatest staining was found. The significance of the footprints was that they were of both the left and right foot, from the same man, and each imprint showed that a nail was missing from each sole.

Believing that Mary had probably been murdered by someone she knew, someone close to her, Haddon then began questioning those who lived around her. The neighbours did not disappoint. They were quick to point the finger in John Danks's direction and the old constable was easily swayed. He arrested Danks some hours later a mile or so from the scene, and after taking him into the Red Lion pub outside Nuneaton charged him with murder.

Danks, of course, denied all knowledge. He had sustained no bloodstaining, had no murder weapon, and argued that he had no cause to commit murder. Haddon did not believe him and after walking him back to the police lock-up had his clothes taken away. Examination revealed that Danks wore two waistcoats, one of which had recently had a button replaced, and a pair of shoes, one covered in dried cow dung. Closer inspection of the shoes also revealed the missing nails on the soles. Haddon took them to the murder scene and after making a second imprint beside that of the first two realised that he had an identical match. There could be little doubt in his mind that it was an open and shut case.

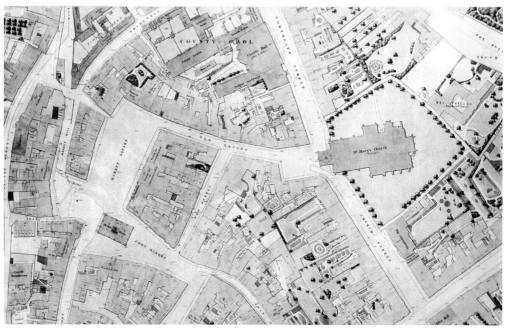

A map showing the location of Warwick prison, 1851. (Author's Collection)

St Mary's Church, Warwick. Danks would have attended his own memorial service here before being executed. (Author's Collection)

So it proved. At the beginning of March 1832 Danks finally confessed. Possibly finding his guilt too burdensome a load to carry he made an impromptu statement to the village curate, Mr King. This found its way to Constable Haddon and after a brief meeting Danks reiterated all he had told the young clergyman for Haddon to record. According to the statement he eventually made he had murdered Mary in a fit of anger.

We walked across the grazing piece by the foot road, and thence to Astley's hovel. We was in the hovel about a quarter of an hour together, when I up with my fist and struck her on the left temple and knocked her down. I fell at her back and cut her once. She hooted very loudly. I cut her again a second time and stopped her hooting. I was quite sure she was done for. I got up, come out of the hovel, and got over the gate. I walked along the road leading to Abbey Street. When I got about one hundred yards from the hovel, I thought I heard a man behind me. I turned myself round but saw no one. I shut my knife and threw it over the hedge into the wheat field. I then made the best of my way to the top of Abbey End and home. I washed my hands and went to bed.

It was a confession that would lead him to the gallows.

The trial opened at Warwick on Friday 30 March 1832 before Sir J. Parke. For Danks it was merely a procession of witnesses, all of whom damned him. The knife he used to carry out the murder was located. Bloodstaining had been discovered on the button the constable had found, also on Danks's trousers; the soles of his shoes were an irrefutable match to the imprints in the field; Mary's daughter Elizabeth confirmed her sighting of him, and his wife offered up no alibi. The only moot point of any note was whether or not Mary Green had been alive when he left her inside the hovel. Had she subsequently struggled to walk the 15yds or so in the direction of home before finally expiring, or had Danks attacked a second time beside the gate and dealt the killer blow there? He argued he had not and the surgeon, Dr Bond, agreed. He told the court that in his opinion she could very well have struggled on alone for a brief time. Constable Haddon disagreed with them both, citing the medical evidence given to the coroner, which showed that despite Danks's insistence that he had cut her twice, there were three cuts to her throat. But at the end of the day it mattered not. The jury returned a guilty verdict after less than five minutes' deliberation. After donning the black cap and passing sentence of death the learned judge gave his final and damning condemnation.

Your guilt appears as clear from the evidence in this case as if we had seen it with our own eyes, that you had induced her to go to the place where you have been before carrying on your wicked intercourse with her, and that she went when she suspected nothing of this kind from you, you there betrayed her cruelly and ungratefully, and committed that crime, which you had before designed in your heart, and inflicted upon her instant death. In the whole course of my experience, I never heard a case in which so much brutality and cruelty has been evinced. . . .

2

A QUESTION OF INSANITY

Spernal, 1842

William Crowley was considered by those who knew him to be quite wealthy. Living at Spernal, which lies on the River Arrow, some 3 miles north of Alcester, he had decided while still a young man to become a farmer, and this course had proved to be extremely profitable. The powerful Throckmorton family, Warwickshire landowners, offered him the tenancy of a farm on the outskirts of the village in about 1790 and later that same year he married. The marriage produced a family of seven before his wife died, possibly in childbirth, in about 1812. With a

Today Spernal is just a tiny hamlet of three or four houses surrounded by farmland.
(Author's Collection)

large family and what was effectively a smallholding to run he quickly remarried and by the late 1830s, when he accepted a second farm, had added another five children to the family roll-call. Life for the Crowleys ought to have been as comfortable as it was prosperous, but while William Crowley had been blessed with wealth he had not been blessed with virtue. He was, by all accounts, a mean-spirited man who had no time for any of his children, except one, and tended to make life thoroughly miserable for most of those around him. It was only to his youngest son Joseph that he paid any attention, and as the boy grew older it was to him that control of the two farms passed. Almost half the family were certified insane and all the daughters, of which there were six, were turned out of the house as soon as they had reached an age at which he deemed them able to care for themselves. Disowned, stripped of all financial resources, they inevitably fell on the parish, which was forced to administer poor relief and on occasion drag Crowley into court to demand that he pay something towards their upkeep. By the end of 1842 only his wife, the youngest son, Joseph, and two servants remained living with him at the farmhouse outside Spernal, and his life was under serious threat from the last member of the family to have been evicted.

James Crowley was 30 years old when he was ordered by his father to leave the house forever. The blood feud had been raging for over two years and when James left, in the spring of 1842, to go and lodge at the blacksmith's house some 300yds away, he promised to kill the old man. It was a threat his father took extremely seriously, although for some strange reason, despite this threat, he still gave his estranged son an allowance of £1 per week, a saddle and a horse for his use. James, now living alone, was far from enamoured of his father's sudden show of magnanimity; rather the reverse. He believed the allowance to be derisory and in an attempt to force an increase published a sixteen-page pamphlet outlining his grievances and detailing the family feud. This piece of polemic rant he then distributed far and wide. It had no effect. Everyone living within a reasonable radius of Spernal knew well enough what William Crowley was like but they also knew what could be done with a weekly allowance of £1. Sympathy was a scant commodity when for most money was in short supply.

While all this was going on William organised a defence against what he believed would be a very real attempt to kill him. Among the labour force working on his farms was a man named William Tilsley. He was a tall, stout man of 20, married with two children and in need of the work. He accepted an offer to become a constable and live in on the Crowley farm when needed. The job he was being invited to take on was essentially that of bodyguard, but he felt he knew the family well and despite the threat posed by James believed it was mostly nothing but hot air. He was very wrong.

On 22 December 1842 Tilsley had his first taste of family conflict. In a sudden burst of anger James stormed into the farmhouse and in a bitter verbal exchange with his father over money reiterated his intention to kill him if things did not change. The old man, incensed by the outburst and intent on the status quo remaining as it was, ordered Tilsley to go seek his son out the following day. He wanted James to see the power he could wield and the threat his newly appointed constable offered. It worked. Tilsley told James in no uncertain terms that he was no longer welcome at the farm and that he was to look elsewhere for his extra money. Had William Crowley stuck to his word then quite possibly the tension between father and son would have eased. Unfortunately, whether influenced by his wife or not, Tilsley's good work was all undone when William offered James an olive branch. It was Christmas and perhaps he felt he ought to offer up the hand of friendship. James was invited to return to the farm on Christmas Day for breakfast.

James, of course, had no intention of burying the hatchet. When he arrived at the farmhouse at a little after eight on a cold Christmas morning any good intentions he had set out with were left on the doorstep. Breakfast was a war of words. Tilsley, who had been ordered to attend, was forced to intervene more than once, much to James's chagrin and breakfast eventually ended in bitterness and acrimony. But this time James was not to be deterred from exacting revenge for what he saw as a life of resentment.

Returning to his lodgings he changed into his Sunday best, collected a shotgun from the cupboard, and stormed back to the farm. Inside the house his mother saw him crossing the fields and without too much persuading forced her husband upstairs. They heard the windows shatter and waited. But outside the trusty Constable Tilsley had also been alerted. Before James could force an entry the big constable ordered him to put his weapon on the ground. James merely turned the shotgun on him and fired. The shot hit the young policeman in the left eye and blew out his brains. He was dead by the time he hit the floor. James then calmly threw the gun to the ground, walked over to the stables, saddled his horse and rode away.

For James there was never going to be any dispute over his culpability and he knew it. As the fatal shot was fired it was seen by at least two other farm labourers who arrived on the scene just too late to influence the outcome. James, of course, had only two options open to him at that point – surrender or run. He chose to do the latter. After arriving in Stratford-upon-Avon by early afternoon he hitched a ride on the mail coach to Shipston on Stour. From there he travelled to Shrewsbury, where he lingered for a few days, certainly long enough to write letters to a woman in Washwood Heath near Birmingham; a woman he had, on occasion, cohabited with and who had no hesitation in handing the correspondence to the police. From there it is believed James travelled to London and then to America where he arrived in early summer.

Meanwhile, back at the farm Tilsley's body was initially carried into a nearby barn where it was later examined by surgeon, William Morris. This was a purely academic exercise on his part as Tilsley had died the instant the shot hit him in the eye. Morris was able to be precise in that view, the damage to the back of the man's head being so extensive that it left absolutely no doubt. He then organised the body's removal to the Marlborough's Head Inn at Studley to await the coroner's arrival.

The inquest opened on 27 December before Stratford-upon-Avon coroner, Mr Hunt. With no doubt as to the identity of the killer the court procedure was one of routine rather than inquiry. Various neighbours testified to being witness to the family feud over the months leading up to Christmas and of the known antipathy between father and son. John Nicholls, 14, and his labourer partner, neighbour Joseph Street, were the two witnesses to the murder and, as expected, their testimony was damning. At the end of the day's proceedings the 'guilty of murder' verdict was returned and the search for James began.

It was never realised that he had taken ship to the American continent. As far as the police were concerned he was presumed to be somewhere in the south of England. They had no reason to believe that he had fled Warwickshire with any significant quantity of money. Everything they knew of the murder suggested it had been a spontaneous act by a disillusioned and angry son who had simply killed the wrong man. In part they were correct. Tilsley had never been the intended victim, but premeditated it most certainly was. James Crowley not only had changed into his Sunday best before returning to the farmhouse that Christmas morning, he had also packed his saddlebags and prepared his horse. But without this intelligence the belief that he could not afford to flee far was reasonable. So was the assumption that he would attempt to disappear in the capital city – it was large enough and dark enough to hide anyone. London's Bow Street police, with this thought in mind issued a statement and description in *The Times* two days after the inquest.

WANTED

James Crowley, 5 feet 9 inches high, stout made, has a mark or seam over one of his eye-brows, good looking, and of gentlemanly appearance, and when last seen was dressed in a dark cloth coat, black shining boots and leather leggings. After committing the murder he absconded, taking with him a horse of the following description: A bright bay, switch tail, nearly thorough bred, one hip down, black legs, ewe-necked, and about 15 hands 1 inch high. A reward of £20 will be paid for apprehension of the murderer.

William Tilsley's funeral took place on the same day. His body had been returned to the family home at Sambourne after the inquest and after a further two days of mourning was carried in procession to the churchyard at Coughton. Large crowds lined the route and according to the *Warwick and Warwickshire Advertiser* it was an extremely moving and painful experience for all. The newspaper also made an appeal to those who had stood in the cold and sung hymns to put their hands in their pockets and donate money; Tilsley had left behind a wife and two children who had no means of support unless they could elicit charity from whatever quarter, a sobering thought and no doubt one local people reacted to, but as the crowds dispersed and the service drew to a close they possibly thought more of justice than benevolence. Unfortunately for the Tilsley family justice was going to be some two years away and for William Crowley, for whom the shot was really intended, it came too late. He died some months later.

Sambourne village green. (Author's Collection)

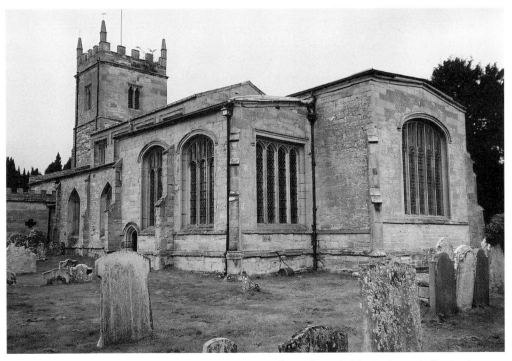

St Peter's Church, Coughton, where William Tilsley's funeral was held. (Author's Collection)

The search for James Crowley began to peter out as the year went on and by the summer of 1843, while he was still obviously a wanted man, there were no active enquiries being made and the case slipped from the public arena. But, inexplicably, as the year drew to a close and his safety seemed assured, he made a decision to return to England. Exactly why is not known. Certainly he never explained himself, but he appeared to have been resolute in deciding the time had come to pay for his passage home, though home was not to be in Warwickshire. When he finally set foot back in England he chose Chester as the town in which to make a new start. It is thought that he took lodgings there in the summer of 1844 and, had he continued to keep a low profile, changed his name and stayed incognito, he would probably have remained free for the rest of his life. Unfortunately James did none of these things. At some point that year it appears he wrote a letter to someone in his family. That letter gave away his location and on 14 December he was arrested and formally charged with the murder of William Tilsley. He made no denial and within twenty-four hours of his arrest had confessed, though without any great detail as to how and why.

The trial opened before Mr Justice Maule almost four months later, on Friday 4 April 1845 at Warwick. When the judge entered the court to take his seat at 9.30 in the morning it was to find every available space occupied and a noisy crowd outside still desperate to find a way in. Such was the interest in the case that people had travelled from miles around both to see and hear the defendant. James Crowley,

Warwick courthouse. (Author's Collection)

however, seemed unperturbed by all the interest, and after a brief glance around the packed courtroom took his place at the bar at a little after 10 a.m. and, in a low voice that betrayed no emotion, pleaded not guilty. During his incarceration he had taken sound advice as to his defence from various quarters, and successfully gained the services of Mr Hill QC, in the hope that a way could be found to keep him off the scaffold. It had been agreed by all parties that the only avenue open to them was insanity. If Mr Hill were able to show that the defendant's actions had been those of a man whose mental state had been severely unhinged then there was a chance, albeit a slim one.

The whole of the morning session was taken up with the prosecution case and a procession of witnesses, all of whom provided compelling and accusing testimony as to James Crowley's seemingly indisputable guilt. So confident was the prosecution counsel that it decided to call a halt to its case as the court adjourned for lunch. Convinced of the validity of its argument, and believing it had produced sufficient evidence in support of its case, it was decided to cut short the witness programme and allow the defence an early opportunity to take the floor. Unfortunately for Crowley, when his barrister rose to his feet at the commencement of the afternoon session he called only one witness.

When Joseph Crowley took the stand on behalf of his brother's defence he was not asked to tell the court what he had seen on that December morning but to outline to the jury as much of his family's history as he could recall. Mr Hill wanted the court to hear of the tragedy that had dogged the Crowley family for the past fifty years and Joseph had been chosen to do the telling. Under careful guidance and a little cajoling he began to tell of the thread of insanity that ran through much of his immediate family.

> My sister Sarah was confined to Henley-in-Arden Lunatic Asylum and after that another . . . My brother John was also affected with insanity. He had tried to stab himself. My sister Maria is not in a sane state of mind. Another sister is affected in the same way; and I cannot speak of the sanity of my sister Mary Crowley. . . .

Under close questioning he went on to tell how the feud between his brother James and his father William had raged for years, and of how all the children had been systematically disinherited. All the land and both the farms had been passed to himself. He told the court there were no shares for any of the other siblings. It painted a bleak picture of life at Spernal and in his closing speech to the jury the barrister made great use of it. Acknowledging the candour and sincerity of the prosecution witnesses, Mr Hill told the jury that he readily accepted James Crowley had shot William Tilsley. There was, he insisted, overwhelming evidence in support of that fact. There was also a reason behind the violence, which was irrevocably tied to the attitude of Crowley's father. But, he asked them, was not James Crowley insane? He went on to reiterate the family history of mental illness and the instability of the father figure.

The entrance to Warwick prison. The archway now bricked up was the entrance and when public executions were carried out the scaffold was erected just outside. (Author's Collection)

The unfortunate prisoner at the bar is a member of a family whom providence has been pleased to afflict with insanity, descending from daughter to daughter and from son to son. . . . Where did he go after committing the act? To America; whence, after remaining some short time, he returned and came to live so near as Chester. Would not a sane man have attempted concealment?

But was it too little too late? The judge certainly thought so and after a two-hour adjournment so did the jury. Despite his counsel's best efforts James Crowley was sentenced to death.

The execution date was set for 18 April but behind the scenes the movement to halt the proceedings and commute the sentence to one of life had already begun. In total ten different affidavits were produced in his defence, a number from people who claimed to have seen Crowley exhibit signs of insanity, some from affluent and influential businessmen who believed an injustice had taken place, and one signed by all the members of the jury calling for clemency. They all fell on deaf ears and at 3 p.m. on 17 April the Secretary of State made his final decision that the execution was to go ahead.

About 2,000 people turned out to watch the public hanging, many having travelled more than a dozen miles to be in Warwick by the designated hour of 10 a.m. It seemed to matter little to the well-dressed prisoner who, after attending a morning service in the prison chapel, walked to the press room where he drank a glass of red wine and held a brief conversation with the prison governor. Once on the scaffold he spoke briefly to the executioner before stepping on to the trap, where at his request the rope around his neck was shifted to a better position, and then he fell to eternity. He died instantly.

3

A CASE OF POISONING

Nuneaton, 1849

For Mary Ball it could be said that life had proved to be extremely arduous and fraught with difficulty and tragedy. But it had not begun that way. Born to a Nuneaton innkeeper in 1818 she had a relatively stable upbringing. When she met the man she eventually married life must have seemed to be on the way up.

Thomas Ball had become a frequent visitor to her father's inn towards the end of the 1830s, helping out with various chores whenever he could. The relationship between the two was probably assured the minute they met, given their similar ages. He was three years younger than Mary and certainly not unattractive. Their subsequent marriage came as no surprise to those who knew them and was probably welcomed by Mary's family. The new son-in-law had the means of self-support; he worked locally as a ribbon weaver, and was young enough to better himself should the opportunity allow. But he also came with a reputation. There appears to have been no room in his life for fidelity – Thomas was known as a philanderer to those around him and Mary perhaps ought to have recognised that.

Initially things went well. The couple eventually moved to Back Street on the edge of Nuneaton and Thomas changed his job and began work on the railway. But Mary grew increasingly unhappy. For her, most of the 1840s were spent in various stages of pregnancy and unfortunately for her most of the children died. This was a time when disease was rife, doctor's services expensive, and medical knowledge scant at best. Personal hygiene was not seen as a high priority, and many childhood illnesses proved fatal. For Mary it must have been a desperate time. Added to her misery was the fact that the marriage was in some difficulty. Thomas continued his libertine ways and the demon drink had

Back Street as it looks today.
(Author's Collection)

begun to take a greater hold on his life than it had previously, though there is no evidence to suggest he was a drunkard. Arguments became the norm. Then Mary met 19-year-old William Bacon.

The Bacons were her husband's employers; how or when she met their son is not known but it certainly became a contentious issue for Thomas. He believed the two were involved in some sort of affair. The young man visited their house from time to time, possibly when he thought Mary would be alone. There seems little evidence to support any serious impropriety but certainly Thomas had, on at least one occasion, watched them through a crack in the wall. What he saw he considered grounds for punishment and Mary was beaten as a result. This led to a further deterioration in their relationship and no doubt Mary had begun to feel victimised and mistreated. As spring came she decided the time had come for her to do something to end the abuse.

During the first week of May, in company with a neighbour, she paid a visit to Mr Iliffe's pharmacy in Market Place, and bought a pennyworth of arsenic. Ostensibly it was for killing the bugs that infested her bedroom, but there was also a secondary purpose – Mary intended to murder her husband. Whether or not such a decision was made days earlier or while she stood in the pharmacy she never explained. But after a jocular exchange with the pharmacist over its use she discovered just how much she would need to kill Thomas. When Mary returned home, some of the arsenic was certainly used for delousing the upstairs rooms, but a sufficient quantity was held back, wrapped in paper, and kept on a kitchen shelf.

On 18 May, Thomas went fishing with a couple of friends. On returning home at about 4 p.m. he complained of feeling unwell. Mary suggested he dilute some salts –

Iliffe & Sons Pharmacy. (Nuneaton Library, PH(N)882/2419)

Market Place, Nuneaton, c. 1900. (Author's Collection)

a common cure for upset stomachs – in a mug of water and pointed towards the paper wrapping, which she had retrieved from a kitchen shelf and placed on the mantel. He did as she suggested. Some two hours later he became violently ill. Mary fetched neighbours to the house but there was nothing anyone could do and by 2 a.m. he was dead.

Mary earnestly believed that the finger of suspicion would never be pointed her way. As far as she was concerned her husband had exhibited all the signs of gastric fever, a classic Victorian medical diagnosis for vomiting, abdominal pain and diarrhoea. When the doctor finally arrived at the house the following morning she expected him to agree when she recalled the symptoms she and her neighbours had witnessed. But arsenic leaves behind tell-tale signs. A heavy metal sold as a white powder in the form of arsenic trioxide, it exudes a garlic odour and signs of haemorrhage to the intestines. The doctor ordered a post-mortem. For Mary that spelled disaster and she did all she could to prevent any further medical intervention, arguing vociferously that an autopsy would be a violation and deeply upsetting to her, the grieving widow. But her show of anguish did nothing to dissuade the doctor, who had realised almost instantly that Thomas had died of poisoning. No doubt it also indicated to him that possibly she was the murderer.

As expected, the examination of the body revealed that between two and three grains of arsenic were found in Thomas Ball's stomach, more than enough to cause his death. Mary denied murder though she never denied having bought the poison. Her defence was simply that Thomas had picked up the wrong packet of salts and she had not been in the room when he did it. Death, she insisted, had been accidental and caused by his hand not hers. Police refused to believe her and she was arrested and charged with murder.

Mary's trial opened on 28 July 1849 before Mr Justice Coleridge, with Mary continuing to maintain that the death was none of her doing, despite the fact that a number of her friends and neighbours were able to testify that Mary had talked of poisoning her husband. The prosecution brought several witnesses to the stand in an attempt to demonstrate intent. There were others equally keen to tell the court of Mary's seemingly irrational behaviour over the post-mortem, and the concern she voiced over what would be found. All of this, insisted the prosecution, were clear indicators of her guilt. Her involvement with William Bacon, the jury were told, had clouded her judgement and caused her to seek her husband's death in order to set herself free. This was powerful stuff and not without a grain of truth.

The defence team, on the other hand, painted a picture of Mary as the successful wife and mother who had simply made a mistake. The arsenic, they continued to argue, had been bought in all innocence and had been placed carelessly on a shelf. She had not seen her husband take the packet but when he had fallen ill she had lied. She had known the minute his illness had begun that it had been caused by poison but did not want to admit as much lest she be held responsible. When the doctor arrived she had tried to hide the fact that he had swallowed arsenic and continued to insist it was gastric fever, simply because she knew she would be blamed.

The jury, however, did not agree and after a two-hour adjournment returned a verdict of guilty but recommended mercy. Mr Justice Coleridge was having none of that. He demanded to know on what grounds they felt mercy ought to be extended. After a hurried consultation they amended the verdict and removed all mention of clemency. Mary Ball was duly sentenced to death.

Imprisoned at Coventry she had only one frequent visitor over the remaining eleven days of her life, the Revd Richard Chapman. As chaplain to the prison he had regular access and ensured he made use of it. A zealot with a fanatical streak, he believed ardently that Mary had to repent of her sins if she was to receive true salvation before her death. But Mary proved a stubborn convert to his rabid religious beliefs. Doubtful over the veracity of his repeated assertion that refusal to acknowledge her guilt meant eventual damnation, she frustrated him on an almost daily basis. Chapman grew ever more incensed by what he saw as nothing other than intransigence. On 4 August, after some seven days of religious debate, he determined that her lack of contrition must be punished. Patience finally exhausted, he grabbed hold of her right hand. In an effort to bring realism into his argument he then forced it over the cell's single candle flame until it burnt, insisting as it did so that when she arrived in hell that was the level of pain she would endure for a hundred years if she did not repent. The manic priest was eventually dragged off by prison guards and duly suspended.

Despite the damage to her hand, Mary continued to deny any involvement in her husband's death, leastways until the day before her scheduled execution. Whether worn down by imprisonment or simply a final acceptance of Chapman's conviction that she had never told the truth, with only twenty-four hours of her life left she requested a meeting with the prison governor. At that final meeting she unburdened herself of the guilt she had carried for almost three months, and confessed. 'I put the

A broadsheet detailing Mary Ball's execution. (Warwickshire County Record Office, C343/LIF(P))

arsenic on the mantel-shelf and told him there was some salts on the shelf, he might take them, they would do him good, though I knew at the time it was not salts; but I thought if he took it himself, I should not get into any scrape about it, for the people would think he took it in mistake.'

On Thursday 9 August Mary made the short walk from the prison in Cuckoo Lane and mounted the steps to the scaffold before a subdued crowd of some 20,000. She stood silently above the trap as the executioner adjusted the noose about her neck, kept her eyes closed, and as the bolt was drawn back fell to her death. Mary Ball was the last woman to be publicly executed in Coventry.

4

THE PRICE OF JEALOUSY

Priors Hardwick, 1872

It is fair to say that Edward Handcock had never been seen by his neighbours as a kindly, even-tempered man: rather the opposite, a man prone to violent outbursts, who could be rational one minute and irrational the next. These periods of anger were always directed at his wives, and by the time he married in the late 1850s there had already been two. The third, Betsy, was probably allotted a deal of sympathy by these same neighbours when she arrived in the village, no doubt unsuspecting of her new husband's destructive past. Had she known of the mistreatment he had meted out to these women over the years perhaps she would have shied away from Priors Hardwick and looked elsewhere for a husband. But she did not, and as a consequence she too found herself on the receiving end of Edward's unpredictable temper.

The reason for his anger and erratic nature was simple enough. Edward Handcock was an insanely jealous man. So for Betsy her sex alone meant that there was no avoiding his frequent outbursts. A smile, a touch, even a few brief words, when directed towards a man, would bring dire consequences if seen by her husband. As the years went by she learned that in her dealings with others caution was to be her byword, and for over twelve years the marriage endured, and produced four children. But at some point towards the end of summer 1872 Handcock's mindless accusations

Priors Hardwick today. (Author's Collection)

of infidelity took on a more serious and threatening tone. Betsy, familiar with the usual jealous outburst and well-aimed punch, began to see a change in his attitude towards her. Up until this time the threats had been merely physical, which meant the two of them would fight inside the house; the outcome was predictable but with no permanent damage done. Suddenly they began to take on a more sinister edge.

Handcock was a jobbing butcher, work which entailed visiting other farms, slaughtering various animals and preparing meat for both trade and consumption. More importantly from Betsy's point of view his trade meant that he held a collection of knives in the house. These knives were kept in a downstairs room along with a grinding wheel used to ensure that they always had a keen cutting edge. For years she had never viewed their presence in the house as a threat to herself. But something had changed; as winter winds blew the summer away she began to fear for her life.

Edward had begun to suspect that she was secretly meeting local police sergeant Thomas Webb. It was an altogether ridiculous suspicion and had no foundation in fact, but Edward never doubted it. On his travels around the local countryside he had also either picked up gossip or witnessed something that convinced him there was a second man with whom she had become involved, named Warren. To the warped mind of Edward Handcock, which required no corroborating evidence, this made his wife a serial adulteress. For Betsy it was a death sentence.

The notion that she had ever had anything to do with either man was complete nonsense. When he finally confronted her in late October 1872 she obviously denied the implied associations. But Edward was not a man easily dissuaded, particularly when he believed his suspicions to be well founded and no logical or convincing argument was going to divert him from murderous intent.

On 13 November at about 4 p.m. he and Betsy had a violent argument, so violent that an hour later she was forced to flee the house in search of parish constable William Sharpe, whom she believed was the only man able to calm Edward down. But on that night of all nights he had left the police house early. For Betsy, his absence was a desperate blow. She had counted on his support when she ran out into the road; to return without it was an incalculable risk but one she had to take.

When she arrived back at the house Edward was upstairs in the front bedroom. In the kitchen were their four children. Walter, the eldest at 13, who had been out working all day and had not witnessed the earlier argument, was sitting at the table; his younger sister, 6-year-old Eliza, was on the floor playing with their other brother and sister. It is doubtful that Betsy realised her husband was upstairs; Walter told her he had heard his father sharpening a knife in the front room. No doubt she assumed that he would have stayed there. Desperate to avoid another explosive row she put a hurried meal together and then, leaving Walter downstairs, ushered the other three up to bed. From the darkness of the other bedroom Edward watched as his wife undressed the children and then tucked each in turn into their beds. As she was about to leave them for the night he ran across the short landing, knife in hand, and struck. The first Betsy knew of it was being stabbed in her left leg.

WEDNESDAY, DECEMBER 18.

Mr. Baron BRAMWELL took his seat at ten o'clock.

THE WIFE MURDER AT PRIORS HARDWICK.

Edward Handcock, 50, butcher, was indicted for the wilful murder of his wife, Betsy Handcock, at Priors Hardwick, on the 13th November last, When asked to plead; the prisoner said, in a very weak voice, "Not Guilty." He was accommodated with a seat in the dock.

Mr. Dugdale and Mr. Chamberlayne prosecuted; and the Hon. E. C. Leigh and Mr. Soden (instructed by Mr. T. B. Sanderson, of Warwick) defended.

Mr. Dugdale shortly stated the facts of the case, and called Walter Edward Handcock, the son of prisoner, who said he was thirteen years of age. At the time of the murder he lived with his father, and worked for Mr. Mumford. On the evening of the 13th of November the witness returned home about five o'clock and found his mother there. He got his tea, and his mother afterwards went out of the house. At this time his father was in the back-kitchen. His mother was absent about half an hour, and during her absence he heard his father whetting a knife. His father then went upstairs, but witness did not observe anything in his hand. When his mother returned home, she undressed her three children, and accompanied them upstairs. A short time afterwards his mother called out to witness from the top of the stairs, "Walter, Walter, he's cutting me." Witness then ran out of the house to call a neighbour, and when he returned he saw his mother lying at the bottom of the stairs, and witness then ran out again, and told a woman named Jane Haynes of what had happened. Before his mother went upstairs, she said to witness, "I expect there'll be a fillelew when I get upstairs." He had not heard any angry words between his parents. The knife and steel produced belonged to his father.

Eliza Handcock, six years of age, was next called. When she stepped into the witness-box the prisoner was visibly affected, and wept bitterly. The nature of an oath was then explained to witness, and she was subsequently sworn, and said she was the eldest daughter of the deceased woman and the prisoner. She remembered being taken to bed with her brother and sister, on the evening of the 13th November. There were two bedrooms—a front and a back one. There was no one in the front room when they got upstairs. Her mother put witness and her brother and sister to bed, and while she was in the room, the prisoner came out of the back room with a knife in his hand. Her father stabbed her mother before she spoke to him. He slipped the knife in one of her legs, and afterwards struck her blows on the right arm and left arm. Her mother then fell on to the bed. Her father pushed her on to the bed,—not the bed witness occupied. Her mother then rose from the bed, and fell down the stairs. Her father remained in the room. Witness remained in bed, and did not call out.

Cross-examined by the Hon. E.C.Leigh, witness said she was lying down in bed when her father struck her mother; she had been up five minutes or so. She did not get up when the blows were struck. Did not know what slipping the knife meant.

Hannah Hart, wife of a labourer named William Hart, living at Priors Hardwick, said her husband resided next door to Handcock. The partition-wall between the two houses was so thin that she could hear nearly everything that passed in Handcock's house. On the 13th of November witness heard the deceased take her children to bed, and shortly afterwards the wall was knocked, and a voice cried, "Hannah, Hannah, I'm stabbed and I'm dying." Witness ran into the house, and found deceased lying at the bottom of the stairs. She obtained some brandy, and remained with the deceased until death took place, about eight o'clock. Witness had occasionally heard

The Warwick and Warwickshire Advertiser *report of 18 December 1872.*
(Author's Collection)

The knife had penetrated her thigh by some 3in. Suddenly in a deal of pain she twisted around to fend him off but was knocked on to one of the children's beds. The two fought briefly, with Edward inflicting more wounds to her arms before she was able to extract herself. Screaming out for her son Walter, who was still in the kitchen, to run for help, she lunged towards the door, fell, and tumbled headlong down the stairs.

Walter needed no second invitation to run for help and within minutes of her body hitting the bottom stair, next-door neighbours, Hannah Hart and her husband, were forcing their way into the house. What greeted them was truly horrendous. The stab wound to Betsy's leg had severed a main artery and blood covered every step on the staircase, was splashed up the walls and had pooled all around her as she lay on the floor. They carried her into the kitchen but there was absolutely nothing that could be done to save her life. Constable Sharpe finally arrived at the house at about 7 p.m. Edward, by now comparatively calm, had stayed upstairs throughout all the commotion, and after disarming himself and placing the knife on a window sill in his children's bedroom, waited to be arrested. The young policeman duly obliged, charging him with the lesser offence of attempted murder. An hour later that was amended to a charge of murder as Betsy finally bled to death on the kitchen floor.

For the next four weeks Edward was incarcerated in Warwick prison while his defence team attempted to piece together a case in mitigation, which they must have realised from the outset would be almost impossible. They also learned very quickly that there was to be no means of exculpation acceptable to the court. The lesser charge of manslaughter, not deemed a capital offence, had already been ruled out.

*Priors Hardwick
church where
Betsy was buried.*
(Author's
Collection)

This meant the only defence available was one of accidental killing – when they entered the courtroom on 18 December 1872 they were going to attempt to show that when Betsy was stabbed Edward Handcock had not intended her death.

The case opened at 10 a.m. before Mr Baron Bramwell. Edward appeared somewhat overawed by the proceedings and pleaded not guilty in a very weak voice; hardly surprising given the number of unfriendly faces that stared out at him from every available space in the courtroom. Large crowds had been gathering around the courthouse since dawn, and long before he entered the dock the doors had been opened for those fortunate enough to obtain entry to seize any vantage point they could. After noting the plea the prosecution took to the floor and for the next half-hour reprised the case and the charge for the benefit of the jury. The case then began in earnest.

Two of Handcock's children, 13-year-old Walter and 6-year-old Eliza, were among the first witnesses called to the stand. Walter told of the events of 13 November – how his mother had left the house early that evening and how, during her absence, he had heard his father sharpening a knife in the next room. He went on to say that, with the benefit of hindsight, he now also believed that he had heard his father go upstairs before his mother had returned, something he had been uncertain of when she had arrived back home. He then described what he saw of the attack, which was very little due to his escape in search of help. Little Eliza, who stood and wept throughout her testimony, corroborated much of what her elder brother had said. Then, visibly distraught, she gave an eyewitness account of the murder of her mother. It was the most upsetting and yet damning testimony the court would hear throughout the trial and it destroyed any hope of mitigating Handcock's actions.

The remainder of the day was spent hearing testimony from the neighbours, those who tried to save Betsy's life and those who were able to tell of Handcock's unpredictable temper. The young police constable explained his movements on the night of the murder and described the subsequent arrest. Surgeon George Bagg gave the results of his post-mortem examination carried out two days after the killing, explaining to the jury that with the exception of her left leg all the wounds sustained by Betsy had been on her arms. He told the court a single stab wound had penetrated some 3 or 4in into the thigh, and although he was unable to be precise, it was likely to have been this wound that led directly to her death. The others were inconsequential and would not have been life threatening. But when the knife had entered her leg it had penetrated so deeply that it had sliced open both a major artery and a secondary blood vessel. The subsequent haemorrhage caused her to bleed to death.

The doctor's evidence was the last to be heard. There were no defence witnesses and the prosecution waived its right at the end of the trial to address the jury.

The Hon. E. Chandos Leigh, who had taken on Handcock's defence then rose to his feet and in a hushed courtroom began his closing argument. In an eloquent speech he accepted that the killing had been as a result of jealousy; that Edward Handcock had always been a jealous man, and that as a result of this irrational emotion his marital relationship had been stormy, even at times violent. But, he argued, he had never shown any inclination in the past to resort to a weapon, nor had he previously made any attempt upon his wife's life. Indeed, he told the jurors, when the medical evidence was carefully sifted it was perfectly clear to anyone who had listened to it that when he struck out with the knife he had never intended murder. Had that been the case, he postulated, would not the knife have struck home in a different part of Betsy Handcock's body? The fact it did not, lent credence to the view that the killing had been accidental. Standing in the middle of the courtroom floor he told the court that when the fatal blow had been struck it had been intended only as a warning, intended to display Handcock's anger but certainly not intended to be mortal.

It was a reasonable stance to take. The medical evidence did appear to support the notion that when Edward stepped into the bedroom clutching a knife his intention had definitely been to stab his wife. But whether that meant he had intended her death was debatable. Because all other wounds had been sustained around the arms and were essentially superficial, murder, it could be argued, had never been intended. If it had, surely the knife would have been plunged into the heart or chest, an area of the body more favoured by almost all attackers as being the key vulnerable area.

The judge, however, did not share the defence's view of unintentional death. After Chandos Leigh had planted the seed of doubt in the jury's mind so effectively, and in the process disparaged the prosecution's charge of murder, the judge directed that the argument for the defence be treated with considerable caution. In a concise reassessment of the salient points raised throughout the trial he brought back into focus a few key facts the jurors were to consider. Handcock had deliberately sharpened a knife at a period of the day when he would not have required it for his work. He had intentionally waited for his wife with the knife in his hand, and had used it without provocation. There was also, he insisted, no evidence that the attack was merely to frighten. Neither were there any grounds to support the notion of manslaughter. At that juncture he ended his summing up. It was enough for the jury to retire for no more than two minutes before returning a guilty verdict. Edward Handcock was then sentenced to death.

The condemned cell in Warwick prison at this time was in the centre of a prison block known as B Division. On the west side of the building was a door leading out into a small square where the scaffold was erected, a distance of no more than 6 or 7ft. According to the *Warwick and Warwickshire Advertiser* it was unique in its design:

An original cell door from Warwick prison. (Author's Collection)

The beam is erected across a small square inlet of the yard, the right and front sides being formed by the boundary walls, and the left by the B Division; the approach being open to the large yard. The beam was supported on two massive iron brackets, and from the centre were suspended two or three iron rings, at the end of which was about four feet of new rope, the thickness of a man's little finger, with a running noose at the end. Immediately beneath was a pit five or six feet deep, with brick sides and steps at one end. Covering this was a wooden platform moved by an iron lever from the steps.

Two appeals were launched in an attempt to save Handcock from ever stepping foot on that platform, both to no avail. At a little before 8 a.m. on 7 January 1873, executioner John Smith entered Handcock's cell, pinioned his arms, and formed the head of a small procession. Less than two minutes later Edward Handcock was dead.

5

OF WITCHES & WIZARDS

Long Compton, 1875

Bachelor James Haywood had lived all his 45 years in the small village of Long Compton. Nestled in a corner of south Warwickshire, the village had grown up around the various outlying farms, with most of its inhabitants employed in one way or another by local tenant farmers and landowners. After leaving school Haywood, like most of his near neighbours, had been happy enough to follow the trend, and by 1875 had established himself as a man with both the skill and physical build to cope with most aspects of life as a farm labourer. Never out of work and never feeling the urge to leave home, he had remained living with his parents and as they aged had taken over the role of key breadwinner.

Life for the Haywoods ought to have been good, and had they not harboured a secret fear of witches and the power they possessed perhaps it would have been. But being born into an isolated community in that part of Warwickshire was not necessarily conducive to contentment and inner well-being. As he passed his fortieth birthday James and his parents became ever more convinced that a coven they had long suspected had finally cast an evil eye in their direction. Coincidentally, at around this time Haywood had begun to feel unwell. Nothing specific, and nothing

Long Compton today.
(Author's Collection)

that had kept him from his work, just a sense that his health was not as good as it ought to have been. But to his parents it was a sure and certain sign that he had been bewitched.

Belief in witchcraft had been prevalent among many of the rural families he had come into contact with throughout his childhood, so much so that by the time James was middle aged his acceptance of the belief went unchallenged. A convert to the notion that witches were the devil's disciples, and as such were in receipt of supernatural powers which they could turn against any individual, seemed a reasonable and rational explanation of his ills. So convinced was he as to the veracity of this argument he began to turn his attention to uncovering the witches he earnestly believed were about to cause his downfall. Urged on by his parents he travelled to Croughton some 12 miles away to consult with the 'water doctor', otherwise known as the 'cunning man of Croughton', who told him he was possessed. Those casting the spells, he told Haywood, numbered between twelve and sixteen witches, but if he wanted to stop them he was to find the ringleader. Here he had no difficulty. Haywood had believed for some time that it had been his next-door neighbour, Ann Tennant, that had cast her evil eye across him. She he blamed for all his minor ailments and he decided she would have to pay.

Ann Tennant was 80 years old and had been a neighbour for over thirty years; her 79-year-old husband John still worked for local farms. Between the two of them they had one daughter, were regular churchgoers and had never been involved in witchcraft. But to Haywood that was no more than a front, a pretence of respectability. Witches, he claimed to know, always went to church, a view he had openly debated in local pubs along with his notion that to stop a witch you had to draw her blood. No one ever took him seriously but Haywood meant every word he uttered.

On 15 September 1875, after what he considered had been the worst month of his life, the opportunity to rid himself of this key witch finally presented itself. In the early evening as he returned home from work he saw Ann Tennant in the village's main street, just as she was leaving her daughter's house. Believing he had been presented with a God-given opportunity for exacting his revenge, he lowered the long-handled pitchfork from his shoulder, which he was returning to the farm, and charged at her. With no time to react she was on the ground before she realised what was taking place. Haywood then stabbed her three times in the legs and before passers-by were able to disarm him had rammed the forks into her head almost as a *coup de grâce*. Carried back to her daughter's house she died shortly afterwards.

Haywood was elated – he had finally rid himself of the main witch from the village and believed himself justified in her death. He showed no remorse and after being arrested by the local constable declared himself vindicated of murder because the killing had been justified by God. Ann Tennant, he told the policeman, was only one of sixteen and he intended to kill all the rest: 'No odds about it; I hope she is dead. There is a lot more I will serve the same.'

The young constable, PC Simpson, believed him to be drunk. So irrational was his behaviour that he could find no other explanation for the attack and for his apparent lack of remorse. He had Haywood taken to the police lock-up at Shipston on Stour. Here he was met by Superintendent Thompson who formally charged him with murder. Haywood continued to show little regard for the old woman he had horrifically mutilated. Instead he told the policeman that he had been under constant attack from a number of witches. At times he became incoherent and abusive and bitter in his condemnation of the village coven he claimed to have uncovered.

At the later inquest, Chipping Norton surgeon, Dr George Hutchinson, told the hearing that Ann Tennant had died as a result of haemorrhage. The pitchfork, while it had done some damage to her head, had done even greater damage to her legs. He told the coroner that both forks had penetrated varicose veins, two on the right leg and three on the left, all below the knee. The resultant damage had been so devastating that nothing could have saved her life regardless of how quickly medical attention had been sought. But Haywood, he told the court, had never exhibited signs of madness in his presence. On the contrary he insisted the man had always appeared rational and sane.

Three months later, on 15 December, James Haywood took his place in the dock before Mr Baron Bramwell at a little after 10 a.m. Throughout his incarceration he had continued to argue the murder was a sinless crime. When he stood in front of the court, took hold of the Bible and pleaded not guilty, he was being sincere. Haywood had never veered away from his view that the killing of a witch was lawful. He had, however, expressed sorrow at her death and claimed that his intention when he had made the attack had been to draw her blood. To kill her, he had claimed, had not been his prime intention but the fact that she had subsequently died had been unimportant, after all she had been a witch. It was a point of law that no longer held credibility in a British courtroom, not that it mattered to Haywood. He earnestly believed that though it may have been unpalatable to the legal system it was justified under the rules and tenets of the Bible.

His defence team, ably led by a Mr Buzzard, were not about to share his belief. For them the argument for mitigation was simple enough, Haywood was insane. They felt that enough corroborative evidence existed in support of this contention to sway the view of any jury. If he was to be saved from the noose then it was his declining mental condition that was to be used as justification for his action. As the trial opened they were of the opinion that this was the only way to save his life.

To this end Buzzard called only three key witnesses. The first was James Anderson, governor of the county prison. He told the court that in his opinion Haywood had exhibited all the signs of mental illness. His belief in witchcraft alone, he contended, was sufficiently irrational to suggest that he had been mentally unhinged for some considerable period prior to the murder. Under skilful probing by the defence counsel Anderson went on to relate a particular event that took place in the prison shortly after his arrest. Haywood, he recalled, had called the governor to his cell to inform him that he had been possessed by a number of witches and that he could prove it. He requested an empty glass phial be left with him overnight. The governor had indulged his prisoner and on the following morning when he returned to the cell had been

Long Compton in the nineteenth century. (Warwickshire County Record Office, PH350/419)

given the phial back again but this time full of what he believed to be urine. Haywood had then pointed to a series of air bubbles and claimed that each rising bubble represented a witch. They, he had pointed out, were sent against him by Ann Tennant, the woman who had ordered the possession. Over the following weeks, according to Anderson's testimony, Haywood's attitude had hardened and shortly before the trial date had been set he had further justified his conduct by quoting from Leviticus: 'A man also or woman that hath a familiar spirit, or that is a wizard, shall surely be put to death; they shall stone them with stones; their blood shall be upon them.' He had also quoted at length from the Apostles, the Acts and from the prophet Micah. All, he had claimed, gave him the right to take the life of a known witch.

The defence of insanity was further reinforced by Dr Parsey, medical superintendent of Hatton Lunatic Asylum. He had been called to the prison towards the end of September and allowed two days' access to Haywood in order to determine his mental capabilities. He told the court that in his opinion Haywood was suffering from delusions and these delusions appeared to confirm that he was insane.

I found him to be of feeble mind, of eager childish manner, and with a loud discordant tone of voice. He took quite a childish interest in the notes which were taken at the interviews, whether the matter was relevant or not, and did not seem to realize in the least the grave nature of the offence he had committed. . . . He considered that he had only killed a witch in order to take

29

her power off him, and prevent his continued illness. He was strongly impressed with the necessity of drawing her blood, because then, he said, the power of a witch ceased. . . . He seemed to think, however, that a witch had no right to live, and when questioned about his authority, said Saul ordered that all wizards and witches should be put out of the land, and that in Leviticus they were all directed to be killed. . . . He enumerated thirteen other witches who lived in the village and who had all his lifetime been putting ailments upon him. . . . He seemed confirmed in his belief in witches from having paid a visit to a 'cunning man' named Manning, who lived at Croughton . . . Manning had taught him by water to find out how they worked upon him. . . .

He went on to tell the court that Haywood was beyond the help of any asylum. In his expert opinion, an asylum could do nothing to reverse the belief, in witchcraft that had shaped the way he both thought and acted. Unlike any ordinary person, he contended, Haywood did not just believe that witches had the power to do evil, he earnestly believed he had seen that power harnessed and set against him. Witches, according to his deep-seated belief, had persecuted him for the whole of his life. That made him both dangerous and unpredictable.

Finally, Dr James Nunn, surgeon at the county prison, took the stand and in a brief testimony concurred with both earlier witnesses, and added that in his opinion nothing would have steered him away from the murder he committed: 'He appeared to be under the popular superstition of the village that he was not able, in consequence of being bewitched, to control his actions. . . . He would not consider an action wrong in the same light as a sane person.'

The judge did not agree. He seemed to have formed the opinion that Haywood had been all too well aware of his actions and pointedly asked the doctor if he agreed that circumstances did exist that could have proved the point.

The Judge: Supposing anyone had stopped him as he was crossing the road to her and said, 'Now, mind you will be hung if you kill that woman', do you think he would have attacked her?

Dr Nunn: I do.

The Judge: I don't.

In his eventual summing up he maintained his stance that Haywood could be whatever the medical profession wanted him to be, but on the day he murdered Ann Tennant he had intended to kill her. That, he told the jury, meant that he was clearly not insane. The killing had been no impulse action. He had discussed his hatred of witches with numerous people in the village, and had made his intentions abundantly clear that he intended to kill them. The only way, contended Mr Baron Bramwell, that he could be mentally ill would be if he had no recollection of events, not that he had a clear memory and knew exactly what he had done.

The jury, however, did not agree. They returned a verdict of not guilty on the grounds of insanity.

6
THE DEADLY MIDWIFE

Ettington, 1897

Elizabeth Brandish was born in 1864 to a good Christian family. Well educated, she chose to become a nurse. By the time she was 20 she had begun a career as a midwife in rural Warwickshire. This meant that she was not able to set up a permanent home as the job entailed an enormous amount of travelling, not only in Warwickshire but also around the counties of southern England. By her mid-20s she had based herself at her brother's house at Drybank Farm, Ettington, where her transient lifestyle was well understood and where she could live for free. Here she was allocated a bedroom of her own, able to come and go as she wished and was a part of a family she knew and trusted. In return for their hospitality she helped out around the farm whenever time allowed, and gave her sister-in-law what help she could with her family of eight. Apparently content with the life she had chosen and not discouraged by the amount of travel she often had to undertake, Elizabeth was seen by those around her as a confirmed and unrepentant spinster. But as she reached her 30th birthday life was about to change.

During 1894 she found herself to be pregnant. In the Victorian society in which she lived and worked a pregnancy outside the sanctity of marriage was ruinous. For

Ettington High Street today.
(Author's Collection)

Elizabeth, had the truth come out, it would have been the end of her career; for her immediate family it would have meant scandal of the worst kind. Fortunately for her she had done a considerable amount of her nursing and midwifery in and around south London. In order to keep her pregnancy secret from all who knew her, well before it would have become glaringly obvious she chose to travel to the village of Aldington, some 6 miles south of Ashford in Kent. Informing her brother that it was a necessary journey and would entail her living in with a patient for some months, she moved in with good friend Harriet Morton. Regular correspondence was sent to the Ettington farm, full of the mundane minutiae of daily life, in order that the subterfuge would not be uncovered. Finally, in May 1895 she gave birth to a son, Rees Thomas Yells Brandish.

With the birth over and her own recovery in hand she knew all too well that at some point she would need to return home and resume normal life. She also needed no reminding that she would never be allowed to do so with an illegitimate child in tow. But Elizabeth was a very resourceful young woman. She had decided long before her arrival in Kent that the child would not be brought up by her. To that end she let it be known that a lone mother was seeking surrogate parents. Without giving away any detail of her circumstances she was hopeful that, for a reasonable maintenance payment, someone would come forward. In July, some nine weeks after her son's birth, her patience was rewarded. Harriet Morton told her of an elderly couple, Mr and Mrs Post, residing in Wye near Ashford who were looking for a child to take in. For Elizabeth it was the best news she could have hoped for, and any fleeting concerns she may have had over their ability to cope because of their age were quickly dismissed when she realised they shared their home with a niece.

When they all met to agree on a payment for her son's upkeep it was the niece who did the negotiating. Elizabeth, who had given her surname as Edwards, left the house in Wye confident in the knowledge that while it was the Posts who wanted a child, it was niece Sarah Urben who was going to do most of the work. After agreeing to a 5s weekly payment, payable monthly by post, the baby was handed over. Then, in order to justify her actions and excuse the lack of future visits, Elizabeth explained to the family that she worked as a nurse in the west of the country, which would necessitate her being absent from Kent for long periods of time. The old couple accepted the situation without argument. Elizabeth, who had no intention of ever returning if she could help it, and constantly aware of the danger of discovery, reassured them that if needed she could be contacted through her sister in any emergency and gave the address of the Red Lion, Little Compton.

By autumn 1895 she was back at Drybank Farm, her family none the wiser, and once again working as a full-time nurse. She continued to base herself at the farm in Ettington, most of her work being in the county, but still travelled south when opportunity allowed. By the summer of 1896 she had succeeded in building a reputation as a humane and extremely compassionate nurse, and her services were in ever-greater demand. This demand eventually took her into Worcestershire where

The Red Lion at Little Compton where Elizabeth had all her mail sent. (Author's Collection)

she was appointed District Nurse and where, in early December that year, she was asked to take over the nursing care of a woman critically ill from pneumonia. This involved her moving into the family's house in the village of Clent where she stayed for over ten days. Unfortunately the woman died, but so involved had Elizabeth become with the family that within months of the death she had begun to build a relationship with the woman's husband.

Police Sergeant Robert Narramore had been with the Worcestershire police force all his working life. After his wife's death he had been left to cope with two daughters, a full-time job and all that life as a widower entailed. Elizabeth stepped in where she could, formed a close bond with the daughters and slowly the relationship between the two grew. Taking lodgings with a Mrs Shilvock, whose house was very close to that of the policeman and his family, added to that sense of closeness and also gave her quick and easy access to his house, though probably not his bed. With a position of some standing in the community it is highly unlikely that he allowed any impropriety, particularly with two daughters at home. Certainly there is no evidence to support the idea of any kind of sexual relationship. But by the summer of 1897 there is little doubt the relationship had strengthened somewhat and Elizabeth began to realise that marriage was a distinct possibility.

While there is no doubt she sought the marriage, she also knew it spelled disaster if she did not do something about the illegitimate baby in Wye. Marriage would force her out of her nursing role, her income would be lost and so would her ability to continue the monthly £1 payments for her son's upkeep. The Post family would surface and make demands, which would force her to admit her son's existence. The marriage would be over and scandal would follow wherever she went. She also knew that if she admitted to having given birth two and a half years earlier the policeman would never marry her. Disclosure would bring outrage from his superiors and opprobrium would follow from all quarters. Eventually she would be shamed into leaving. So she decided upon a plan of action designed to rid her of the problem forever.

Towards the end of August 1897 she wrote a letter to Sarah Urben in which she announced that it was her intention to remove her son from Wye. She went on to say that her brother had agreed to take the child in at Drybank Farm and that she would travel south within two weeks to collect him. She eventually arrived at the house in Kent, dressed as a nurse and carrying only a mackintosh, on 8 September. It was the first time she had seen her son since the handover some two years earlier. The meeting went well enough, but Sarah and her aunt and uncle expressed some concern at the little boy's departure. He had settled in at Wye and the Posts had grown extremely fond of him and were reluctant to let him go. But they had no status in law that would have allowed them to hold on to the child, and Elizabeth was extremely persuasive. She explained that there were eight other children at the farm, a ready-made family, and that her son would have children of his own age around him. She also cited her own lack of funds as a secondary reason, and that she had also been given an opportunity to go into business with a sister. It seemed sensible, she told the couple, that if she were to take up the chance of this small business her son ought to be with her. There was no arguing against it.

Elizabeth stayed in Kent for two days. On 9 September she travelled into Ashford where she paid a visit to a furniture dealer. After some deliberation she bought herself a round tin bonnet box. But this was no ordinary bonnet box. Elizabeth spent some considerable time choosing not only a box that was larger than the average and with a handle for carrying, but also one that could be locked. The shop assistant sold her a padlock for that express purpose. She then took the box to Ashford railway station where she placed it in left luggage until the following day.

On 10 September, with her son smartly dressed in a sailor outfit and a fawn jacket with large pearl buttons, and after refusing to take any other clothing for her son, she said her farewells to Mr and Mrs Post. While all this was taking place Sarah Urben, whom she had told of the box purchase the previous evening, forced on Elizabeth a small brown paper parcel and told her to put it into the box at the railway station. If she had bought luggage, she insisted, then she had to take some of the little boy's nightwear. The package, which Elizabeth tried hard to refuse, was made up of a couple of nightdresses, a pair of drawers, two pinafores and a frock, all of which, Sarah contended, would be needed, as would some help in carrying it. Despite Elizabeth's protestations Sarah, no doubt still reluctant to let the boy go, volunteered to accompany the two of them to Ashford station. After two years of sharing a large part of her life with young Rees there was a genuine unwillingness to let him go too easily. Sarah wanted to stay with the boy until the very last moment. After raising strong objections to the suggestion, Elizabeth eventually backed down and acquiesced. They all arrived on the London-bound platform around mid-morning. Elizabeth bought third-class tickets to Charing Cross and after retrieving the tin box, placed inside both the parcel and her mackintosh as Sarah had suggested. There followed another, but this time final, emotional farewell before mother and son boarded the train and then a tearful Sarah watched until the train had disappeared into the distance.

From Charing Cross Elizabeth travelled to Euston. Here she left the station and the two of them went into a coffee house in nearby Drummond Street. There she stayed until early evening and when she finally emerged on to the street was hopelessly drunk. Local woman, Ada Turner, saw her staggering around Euston Road with her son and believed her to be ill. Dressed as she was in her nurse's uniform and with a small boy in tow added to the woman's sense of alarm. Drunks were a familiar sight but not dressed as professional women. Ada believed that Elizabeth was either seriously ill or had been given drugs. The coffee shop had an unsavoury reputation and it had not been the first time she had seen someone leave it in a distressed state. Convinced Elizabeth had been mistreated in some way or another she decided to help. Flagging down a cab she bundled her and the little boy into the back and sent them off to Albany Street police station.

Police Sergeant Cockshaw met the cab as it arrived outside and his experienced eye told him instantly that the woman who clambered out of it was simply roaring drunk. Elizabeth was coherent but unsteady. He brought her into the station along with her son and organised a quick check-up by the police doctor. He concurred with the sergeant, and after being allowed some time to compose herself Elizabeth eventually managed to tell them that she had consumed a number of brandies, but refused to explain why. Other than giving her name as nurse Elizabeth Edwards, en route with her son to Bletchley, she said very little. With no offence committed the police held her at the station until about 8 p.m. By that time the surgeon agreed she had sobered sufficiently to be allowed to leave, but Sergeant Cockshaw, a careful man, organised an escort in the shape of Policewoman Elizabeth Pickles. She was tasked with ensuring the pair arrived safely at Euston railway station and were put on the first train to Bletchley. But by the time they arrived at Bletchley railway station, which was about 9 p.m., it was too late to catch a connection into Warwickshire until the following day. Somewhat reluctantly, therefore, Elizabeth booked into the nearby Railway Hotel for the night.

Rising early next morning and without breakfast she, the little boy and her tin bonnet box were back on the station platform by 8 a.m. After consulting the timetable she bought tickets for the 8.20 a.m. to Blisworth, to the west of Northampton, a journey of around forty minutes. Here, after apparently missing her connection to Stratford-upon-Avon, she was forced to stay for the whole of the day. In fact it was 4 p.m. before she was able to continue her journey and only then as far as Towcester. There she had another three-hour wait kicking her heels in a waiting room before the last train of the day to Stratford-upon-Avon at 7.19 p.m. Young Rees, understandably fretful, had by this time become quite a handful. There was little Elizabeth could do to pacify him and just before boarding the train changed her third-class ticket to a second-class one, which would give her the use of a compartment rather than an open carriage. Citing her son's fractious behaviour as the reason for the change, she told the stationmaster that it would be better if they travelled the remainder of their journey away from other passengers. He was sympathetic. On duty since the two had arrived at Towcester he had witnessed for himself just how contrary the boy had become the longer time had gone on. When the train finally arrived, conscious of her difficulty he offered to carry her tin box while she carried her son and put the two of them into a compartment alone.

The 7.19 from Towcester to Stratford-upon-Avon was no express. Its journey was slow and its route circuitous. Train guard, John Days, who travelled the route daily and knew Elizabeth by sight, had been told at Towcester that a nurse and her son were travelling in a second-class compartment. A diligent man, John Days liked to know where his passengers were and to that end left the train for a moment when it arrived at Blakesley, its first stopping point. A quick walk along the platform (there were no corridors on trains at this time) and a glance into the second-class carriage confirmed that she and the boy where still where they had been put and he left them alone. From Blakesley the train then stopped at Morton Pinkney, Byfield, Fenney Compton, Kineton and Ettington. At each stop John Day left the train to help passengers and cleared the platform before signalling to the driver to move off. After that initial check he had no cause to go near the second-class carriage until the train's arrival at Kineton at 8.15. He then noted that Elizabeth had pulled down the window blinds but paid no serious attention. It was dark outside and not unexpected. Ten minutes later the train

Ettington railway station, c. 1900. (Warwickshire County Record Office, PH352/73/43)

stopped at Ettington's platform. He saw Elizabeth step out of the carriage with what he thought was a bulky parcel beneath a mackintosh flung over her right arm and went over to retrieve her tin box from the compartment. He never saw a child.

Elizabeth, who had been the only person to leave the train, then walked to the station's waiting room, went inside and sat down. Railway porter, William Hooten, whose job it was to check all passenger tickets, watched from the end of the platform. Suspicious as to why she had chosen the waiting room rather than the exit he followed her. When he walked into the small room and requested her ticket, Elizabeth was sitting in a corner, partly hidden in shadow. The tin box was at her feet and laid across her lap a parcel, which the porter later described as being oblong in shape and about 2ft in length. Suddenly believing he had walked in upon a mother breast-feeding her child he ignored his own request, did a smart about-turn and left. But he did not wander off very far. Within a minute or so Elizabeth, perhaps startled by his interruption, re-emerged on to the platform and made for the exit sign. But the efficient porter was not about to allow a passenger out before they had given up their ticket. He caught up with her as she was about to leave. After a bit of a juggling act with the parcel she produced the tickets she had bought in Towcester and asked if he would carry her tin box to Drybank Farm. The porter refused but offered to take it over on the following morning. Elizabeth declined the offer, said she needed it that night and left. Hooten saw no child, but then neither would he have expected to, realising at last who she was. Elizabeth had been a regular visitor to her brother's house over the years and he knew her to be single.

The walk to the farm was approximately a mile along an unlit road. After some three-quarters of a mile there was a wooden bench. Elizabeth knew it well and when she found it that night she stopped. Ettington parcel-carrier John Heritage, out on his Saturday evening delivery round, found her there at a little after 9 p.m. Recognising her as George Brandish's sister he stopped his cart and offered to take her up to the house when he had finished. She agreed and according to his later testimony he loaded up her tin box, which he claimed was heavy, and she carried a parcel – but not the bulky, 2ft oblong package the porter had seen. When he helped Elizabeth into his cart she clutched a small brown paper parcel no more than 1ft square. After completing his deliveries he dropped her at the farm just before 10 p.m.

While the visit to Drybank Farm was unannounced it was not necessarily unexpected. Elizabeth had spent a week's holiday there at the end of August and when she had left she told her sister-in-law Louisa that she may well be back in early September. As she treated the house as a home, turning up at all hours had never been a problem. The bed was always made and her bedroom kept unoccupied. Brother George carried her tin bonnet box up to her room and after a light supper everyone retired to bed. On the following morning Elizabeth had her brother bring a large tin trunk down from the attic. The trunk was hers and she had used it on occasion if she were travelling because it was large enough to carry as much of her wardrobe as she needed. Informing the family that she intended returning to her digs at Clent on the following day, Monday, but needed to take some linen with her, the trunk was left in her bedroom. On Monday morning Louisa helped her pack and watched as she placed the tin bonnet box inside the larger trunk.

Elizabeth and her trunk arrived back in Clent later that day, 13 September. Her landlady Mrs Shilvock had it brought into the kitchen and before Elizabeth arrived back at the house she and a neighbour carried it upstairs. Yet, just two days later, Elizabeth announced that she was returning to Ettington and taking the trunk with her because she had left something behind that she now needed. Exactly what this was, despite some probing questions by her landlady, she refused to explain, so, on 16 September she boarded another train with the large trunk and arrived back at her brother's house. She stayed for twenty-four hours then took the trunk back to Clent. While all this was going on she also found time to write a letter to Sarah Urben in Wye, to appease her concerns over little Rees leaving Kent. Elizabeth was conscious that Sarah may begin to ask a few pertinent questions if she were not made to believe that all was well.

But Sarah's concerns were not to be so easily assuaged. Towards the end of September she wrote a letter to the vicar of Ettington, Mr Biggs, asking that he check up on a child supposedly living at Drybank Farm. She furnished the vicar with sufficient detail for him to identify the boy easily, and fully expected him to respond with a brief update on his state of health and well-being. When she received an angry retort from Elizabeth lambasting her for involving a third party Sarah went straight to the Ashford police. They in turn notified Stratford-upon-Avon, and after enquiries it was revealed that Elizabeth had returned to Clent. Worcestershire police were asked to investigate.

For Elizabeth this was a disaster. Superintendent Alfred Pugh arrived at Mrs Shilvock's doorstep on 22 October. After informing the curious landlady that the interview was to be conducted privately he took Elizabeth into a small back room and asked pointedly if she had a son. Embarrassed, humiliated and most definitely scared, Elizabeth had little choice but to confirm that she did. After explaining that Sarah Urben had expressed serious concerns as to the boy's whereabouts and well-being he demanded that she tell him where he could be found. Elizabeth at first refused. She claimed it had nothing to do with either the police or people in Kent no matter how concerned. But Superintendent Pugh was not easily dissuaded. He told Elizabeth in no uncertain terms that her feelings in the matter were of no consequence; he had been sent to discover the boy's whereabouts and would not be leaving until he did. An argument of sorts followed but Elizabeth was no fool and realised quickly enough that she would have to furnish the policeman with something. What she told him was a bizarre story of adoption, that while plausible was somewhat vague and indeterminable:

I met a woman on Clent Hill this summer, not long before I went away at the beginning of September, and was talking about children. Some had them that did not want them. She said she would like to adopt one. I said I know of one, and that I could get it for her. She agreed to take it, but no one was to know anything about it. I saw her several times. I met her in Birmingham at the station. She went to Ashford in the same train, but not in the same carriage. I went to Wye and she stayed in Ashford. The next day I went to Ashford and saw her again. While at Ashford I bought a tin box. We came on to London but the woman would not take it that day. She travelled to London in the same train but not in the same carriage. She told me to stay in London but I did not, but came on to Bletchley. The next day I took train to Stratford-on-Avon, as I did not know where she was to come to me. I saw her at Towcester and she told me to get into another compartment, and she took the child. Then I went on to my brother at Ettington. I do not know who the woman was, or where she came from, but I believe she came from Birmingham. I did not tell my brother anything about it and he did not know I had a child. I came from my brother's on the Monday, and went there on the Saturday. . . . I went to meet the woman in Birmingham but she did not come to me as promised at Snow Hill.

Elizabeth went on to describe this mystery woman as being aged about 40 or 45, rather tall, respectable-looking with a fresh complexion. She told the superintendent that the whole arrangement had involved no money changing hands and the woman had met all her own expenses. It is doubtful that he believed a word of it.

Two days later Mrs Shilvock left her house in her tenant's capable hands as she had to go away for a few days. Left alone for the first time since her return from Kent Elizabeth lit a fire. Unfortunately for her the fire made too much smoke, neighbours watched, and by the end of the month the ash pile at the bottom of the garden was being sieved by police. It yielded up a solitary, large, smoked pearl button.

This had a serious impact on her relationship with Robert Narramore, the man Elizabeth had one day hoped to marry. As a sergeant working in the police station responsible for carrying out the enquiries into Rees Brandish's disappearance, Narramore had been automatically included in the initial investigations. As a result Elizabeth had also been forced to admit the illegitimate birth to him. But it would appear that Narramore was quite happy to believe that the child had been given away. Whatever misgivings he may have had he never shared them. But after the discovery of the button and the failure to find the mystery woman who had taken the child, things began to change. He was warned off his relationship by senior police officers who had begun to suspect that Elizabeth Brandish had committed murder and did not want one of their own involved. Narramore took a step back and began to re-evaluate his involvement. In early November Elizabeth wrote him a letter. It was never posted but discovered still in her handbag when she was arrested on 9 November. In it she apologised for the trouble she felt she had brought to both him and his daughters. More importantly she also stated that: 'My one great trouble is that my brother and his family might be brought into trouble through me and I swear that they knew nothing of my affairs.'

The significance was not realised until 13 November, four days later, when, having tired of searching for a mystery woman the police decided instead to dig up the gardens at Drybank Farm. At 1.30 p.m. in a vegetable patch 15yds away from the farm front door they discovered the body of a child. It lay some 1ft beneath the soil surface, was in a foetal position with its knees pressed hard into the chest and covered in quick lime. After being carried to the Chequers Inn a medical examination confirmed that it was male, 34in tall, well developed and approximately 2½ years in age. The lime had caused severe decomposition and there were no remaining facial features. If this was the body of Rees Thomas Yells Brandish then, according to police, those lines taken from Elizabeth's letter damned her. She could not have expected trouble to descend on her brother and his family had she not known when she put pen to paper that a body lay in their garden. Elizabeth Brandish was charged with murder.

At 10 a.m. on 15 November an inquest into the child's death opened in a room adjacent to the one in which the body had been laid after its discovery. Coroner Theo Christophers ordered that the inn remove one of its internal partition walls before he began so that the crowd, which had been gathering since dawn, would be able to come in from the street. Elizabeth Brandish, much to the disappointment of all those who had stood outside in the cold, had chosen not to attend and remained in Warwick gaol.

Sarah Urben had been brought from Kent and was the first to take the stand. She told her story succinctly, explained the arrangement she and her aunt and uncle had made with the child's mother, described the morning of his departure from Wye and told the court that the boy had been in rude good health except in the early part of August when he had suffered a bout of whooping cough. The various railwaymen

The Chequers Inn at Ettington where the inquest was held. (Author's Collection)

gave evidence of having seen Elizabeth at various times and places between 8 and 16 September. George Brandish and his wife Louisa described how and why their home at Ettington had become her home. And a number of witnesses gave evidence, not only of having seen her at various points and times on her journey from Kent, but more importantly, of what she had been carrying. However, the most important witness of the day was William Walter Fenton, doctor of medicine and the man who had carried out the post-mortem.

He told the court that the body had been buried with the head pressed into the chest and the legs pressed into the abdomen. The lime that had been thrown over it, apart from destroying all the facial features, had also obliterated any external marks to the body. What was left were most of the internal organs, all the teeth and much of the hair. What he had been able to conclude was that the child had probably died after pressure had been applied to the chest area. This conclusion was borne out by the fact that after examining the chest and throat he was able to confirm that the trachea, larynx and gullet showed no signs of a foreign body or anything that could have caused choking. But there was a considerable amount of congestion of the subcutaneous tissues at the front of the neck and the thorax, which was in marked contrast to other body tissues. Furthermore, this congestion was also found in some of the muscles around the chest. He went on to tell the court that in his opinion this congestion was a direct result of pressure being applied to the neck and chest area prior to death, though he was not able to confirm that it had actually caused the death.

Under questioning from the jury he also confirmed that it would have been possible for the boy to be placed into the tin bonnet box within a short time of that death and if that had been so, he told them, it would also explain the position in which the body lay in the ground. Rigor mortis would have set in within four hours. The body would have become rigid for up to thirty hours, which meant that had he been inside the tin box and taken out during this time his body would not have been pliable, hence the position in which it lay. After a number of other questions related to his findings the coroner asked if he had tested for poison. The doctor confirmed he had not and so, at that point, the coroner adjourned the inquest until those tests had been carried out. Bizarrely, as he brought the hearing to an end, and with tests still to do, he also gave permission for the body to be released for burial.

Elizabeth made a brief appearance in court at Stratford-upon-Avon three days later and was remanded for a further week. The coroner's court reconvened on 22 November at the Reading-Room, Ettington, where space allowed for a greater audience to be admitted to the proceedings. The hearing was relatively short. The tests for poison had not been concluded and according to Guy's Hospital, London, where they were being carried out, it would take a further two or three weeks. So Dr Fenton was asked to give more details as to the child's body and its age. He told the coroner that the boy had been buried as instructed by the last hearing and then exhumed in order that even more tests could be carried out, which had allowed a little more time for examination. This secondary investigation had satisfied him that the child, as he had initially believed, had died when 2 or 2½ years old, had quite possibly been laid inside the tin box on his back before rigor mortis set in, had weighed approximately 2 to 2½st and that death had occurred some six to ten weeks earlier, which placed it between 4 September and the post-mortem on 14 November. As Elizabeth Brandish had been living in Clent without interruption since her last visit home on 16 September this testimony was extremely damning.

It got considerably worse after the resumed inquest sat for the last time on 13 December, despite test results from London which showed that there had been no poison in the child's body. In the intervening weeks other tests had been carried out on his hair. Before Rees Brandish was given over to his mother, Sarah Urben had taken him to have a haircut and then saved some of the hair as a memento. This was checked against that found on his body and it matched. She had also confirmed that the little boy had sixteen teeth and exactly where these teeth were inside his mouth and once again this matched exactly. After a thirty-minute adjournment the jurors returned a verdict of wilful murder against Elizabeth.

After a number of further remands she was finally brought before Stratford-upon-Avon County Police Court three days later. The court sat throughout the day and heard various testimonies from those who had attended the coroner's court. It was a foregone conclusion. The court simply had to decide if there was a case to be answered and whether Elizabeth Brandish ought to be sent to the New Year Assizes. Clearly there was, and as expected she was ordered to stand trial in the spring of the following year.

This long-awaited and much-publicised trial opened on Thursday 10 March before the Lord Chief Justice, Lord Russell. For several days before the trial people had been queuing at the Under-Sheriff's office in Warwick to apply for tickets that would admit them into the public areas of the courtroom; most of them were women. Unfortunately the court only had room for around sixty people in the public gallery, which meant hundreds were thronged around Northgate on a bitterly cold and foggy morning with no hope of admittance. But such had been the press coverage, both local and national, that feelings ran high and understandably people wanted to see the woman accused of so vile a murder. By ten in the morning the whole building was effectively under siege. Undeterred by the appearance on the court steps of Warwickshire's police superintendent, Evans, and his announcement that no one without a pass would be allowed in, they simply surged towards the doors as they opened. Chaos followed with people literally fighting their way into the courthouse. Press men fared little better. With over thirty newspaper representatives and only ten allocated seats, they were forced to depend upon the profile of their respective newspapers being of adequate standing to get the court ushers to allow them access at all.

Lord Russell, seemingly oblivious to the mayhem, took his seat at a little before 10.30 a.m. Before commencing the morning's events he allowed himself an extensive dip into the snuff box he was renowned for carrying into court, then signalled to the Clerk of Assize, Mr Coleridge, to call the defendant to the bar. Elizabeth Brandish, smartly dressed in her nurse's uniform, her blonde hair hidden beneath a small, closely fitting bonnet, pleaded not guilty in a loud clear voice. The jury were then sworn in and as a hush fell about the room prosecution counsel, Mr J.S. Dugdale QC, rose to his feet and for the next one and a half hours outlined the case for the Crown. He ended his résumé by instructing the jury that they were allowed no latitude in a murder case. Murder was a capital offence. They would only be allowed to convict or acquit.

The prosecution case from the outset was simple enough. It was contended that Elizabeth had planned to murder her son back in July 1897. At around that time marriage to Police Sergeant Narramore had been raised and looked extremely likely. Elizabeth, it was argued, knew that marriage would never take place if the existence of an illegitimate child was discovered. She therefore travelled to Kent to collect the boy and murdered him in the second-class compartment of a train as it travelled between the stations of Blakesley and Ettington. The body had been concealed inside a tin bonnet box, taken to her brother's house, a man who knew nothing of the boy's existence, and finally buried in the front garden. The contentious issue, according to the prosecution counsels' opening, was whether or not she had kept the body in the tin box for several days. They believed it to be highly likely that she had and that the

CHARGE OF MURDER AT ETTINGTON.

THE ACCUSED IN THE DOCK.

On Wednesday night Detective-Inspector Ravenhall, the head of the county detective force, stationed at Aston, brought to Stratford a prisoner, named Elizabeth Brandish, aged 33, a single woman, who was arrested on warrant charging her on suspicion with the wilful murder of her illegitimate son, aged two years and three months, in the parish of Ettington, on September 11th last. The prisoner was lodged in the cells at the County Police-station in Guild-street for the night, and was brought up on Thursday morning before Mr. Henry Holtom at the county police-station. The police were represented by Superintendent Evans, of Shipston, and Superintendent Lambourne, of Stratford, in addition to Mr. Ravenhall. The prisoner appeared rather over the age stated in the warrant. She was dressed in a uniform of the kind worn by hospital nurses, and is a fair woman, under the medium height, with regular features and was perfectly collected in manner. She is a single woman.—Superintendent Evans said he could not go into the facts of the case that morning, as he should want witnesses from distant parts of the country, and he should only ask for a remand.—Inspector Ravenhall deposed that he was accompanied by Superintendent Pugh, of Stourbridge, and arrested the prisoner at Clent, at the house of Mrs. Shilcock. She asked for the warrant to be read a second time, and then said, "I am ready to go with you."—Prisoner said in court she had no questions to ask, and was willing to be remanded as the magistrates thought fit.—She was remanded for a week to Warwick gaol. The police have issued the following circular, which gives the material features of the story so far as it is known to them up to the present: "On or about the 11th September, 1897, a male child, aged two-and-a-half years, mysteriously disappeared from a train between Towcester and Ettington stations, on the East and West Junction Railway, between 7.19 p.m. and 8.18 p.m. The child was in the custody of its mother, Elizabeth Brandish, who was dressed in the garb of a nurse, and was seen to enter a second-class railway compartment at Towcester station. When the train arrived at Ettington station the woman Brandish alighted, she then had no child, and was carrying a parcel wrapped in a white material, which is supposed to have contained the dead body. Description and clothing the child was wearing at the date of disappearance:—Blue and white straw sailor hat, with navy blue band; grey dress, gathered in a yoke; white flannel petticoat; also pink petticoat, unbleached calico shirt, black socks, and a pair of laced shoes, with tin on toes; light-brown jacket, with sailor collar, piped with black cord, and rather large pearl buttons." The police are anxious to discover the body, and ask that special enquiries be made in every police district, and information to be sent to Superintendent Evans, of Shipston-on-Stour. It is understood from independent inquiries that up to Thursday night no clue had been obtained as to the whereabouts of any body supposing the crime to have been committed. The accused, at the time of her arrest, was employed as a nurse in maternity cases in the village of Clent, by a committee of ladies. When she visited Ettington last September it was for a holiday. She has relatives there, but is not a native of the place.

A newspaper cutting from 13 November 1897.
(Warwickshire Advertiser and Leamington Gazette)

box had been secured inside a tin trunk and taken to her lodgings at Clent. There, Mr Dugdale asserted, she had probably intended to bury it in her landlady's garden but had not been able to create the opportunity. Instead the body had been brought back to Drybank Farm where it was eventually found.

It was an extremely strong case and throughout the next two days a parade of witnesses, all of whom had testified at the magistrate's and coroner's hearings, gave it credence. The case for the defence appeared to weaken almost with every hour that passed. There was little the lawyers could do to counter the witness accounts of Elizabeth's movements over the days in question. So they accepted them for what they were. Instead, with a defence built around her contention that she had given her son away to a stranger, they attempted to cast doubt on the evidence that placed her with the child after Towcester. Their whole defence revolved around the fact that it was there that the child was handed over and that when railway guard John Days, who was the principal prosecution witness, claimed to have seen her seated inside the carriage at Blakesley railway station, he was wrong. As to the body in the garden they simply cast doubt first upon its identity and secondly upon the manner of its death.

The defence strategy was to attack the evidence of three key witnesses – John Days, Police Sergeant Narramore and Dr William Fenton. Of the three, Days's testimony proved the most obdurate and difficult to break down. He refused to budge from his claim that he had seen her and her son in the same railway carriage. Nothing the defence raised deflected him from this conviction. In the case of the policeman, however, they had more luck. Under cross-examination by barrister Mr Hugo Young, the defence succeeded in showing that despite the prosecution's insistence that impending marriage had driven Elizabeth to murder, no marriage had ever been discussed. On the stand Narramore told the court that while he considered it likely they would have married, he had never asked her or raised the subject with her. This was their first breakthrough. The policeman's testimony destroyed the motive.

Northgate, Warwick, where crowds massed on the morning of the trial. The building itself is the outer wall of Warwick prison. (Author's Collection)

Ettington Main Street, c. *1900.* (Warwickshire County Record Office, PH352/73/8)

Dr Fenton was also forced to admit that despite all his earlier evidence and the assumption that the child had been murdered was erroneous. From the witness box he agreed he had never examined a body that had decomposed to such an extent, nor had he ever seen injuries of the type he claimed were caused by violence. Again under expert cross-examination he was forced to admit that the injuries could have occurred after death and that he could not be precise as to time of death, and that there was nothing in his own evidence that would support an allegation of murder. It was a major breakthrough for Elizabeth Brandish.

At the conclusion of the trial Mr Young took the floor and in a speech lasting two hours cast serious doubt upon the prosecution's case. He told the jury no evidence had been produced in court to substantiate the claim that his client had committed murder:

If she had desired to kill the child and dispose of the body, she had plenty of opportunity in travelling alone from Ashford to Charing Cross with it. As to the evidence as to cause of death what you have heard from Dr Fenton was not worthy of being acted upon in a case of life and death. It was the first time he had ever had a case of this kind to examine, and to express an opinion upon. The marks on the body might have been caused after death; and if caused after death it was immaterial. . . . Even taking the assumption of the crown that she concealed the body, you must remember that with a person who had an illegitimate child, the desire of concealment was great during its life, and greater still after its death. I do not suggest the prisoner has given truthful accounts of the child's whereabouts; but you must consider the desire for concealment in cases of this sort. . . . Assuming that this was her child's body, and that she buried it, it did not follow at all that violence was inflicted upon it by her. . . . A jury must have submitted to them evidence upon which they could rely before they could come to a conclusion that this was the body; and it was not enough to say, looking at the circumstances of the whole case, that in all probability this was the body. How was it suggested that this was the child? The crown put forward four things. It was about the same age and same sex, and it had the same number of teeth and similar hair to the missing child. The first two things might be put on one side altogether, and the evidence as to the teeth and hair only went to show that they were similar to what were usually found on a child of that age.

Young went on to destroy the motive of pending marriage, and raised the possibility that Elizabeth Brandish, after giving her child away to a stranger, had been forced to take it back after its sudden death. If that were true, he argued, she would have been compelled to dispose of the body somehow. So the fact a child's body had been discovered illegally buried did not automatically mean it had been murdered.

It was a powerful argument but not one the Lord Chief Justice felt inclined to accept. In his summing up he told the jury that they had to examine the medical evidence in relation to the body and ask themselves whether it was the body of Rees Brandish. He pointed out that it was about the same age, height, had the same

Kineton railway station, 1871. (Warwickshire County Record Office, 352/102/50)

colour hair, same number of teeth and same weight. If they agreed that it was the little boy then it followed that Elizabeth put it into the ground. If they accepted that then they must question how he died and also how his body was taken from the train. Had she carried it in the bonnet box? If she had would she have done so had the child died of natural causes? He continued to raise such questions for over three hours, then left the jury to their deliberations. Three and a half hours later the jury sent a message to his chambers to inform him that they were unable to reach a verdict. At five in the afternoon they filed back into the court and were released from service. Elizabeth Brandon was returned to prison to await a retrial.

On the following day Birmingham newspapers published an account of the jurors' deliberations in which they stated that only one jury member had held out against a guilty verdict. They accused one man of having purposefully held out against all his fellow jurors because he did not believe in capital punishment. The man was George Euston of Claverdon, a member of Stratford-upon-Avon's Board of Guardians. This in itself was a serious offence. Wilful disobedience to the oath was how the law termed it and any juror admitting to it put themselves at some jeopardy. Keen to elicit the truth, and recognising a great story when they saw one, press men descended on his home desperate to obtain an interview. It took some persuasion but eventually Euston relented and agreed to go public.

He denied that he had been obdurate for altruistic reasons. He claimed he had been perfectly willing to return a guilty verdict despite his own serious reservations as to the effectiveness of the law in such cases. The problem, he insisted, was not one of conscience but of fact. He told the gathered press men that in order for him to agree with the other eleven jurors the prosecution needed to have proven a number of crucial points:

The chief points to which I directed my attention were: the identity, the cause of death, did the accused dig the hole in the clay soil of Drybank Farm, as alleged? Did she carry the body about between Drybank Farm and Clent in the hot weather prevailing at the time? Could she have effectually concealed the body in the mackintosh at Ettington station? Was the evidence of the guard Days to be accepted without careful consideration? I told the others if they could convince on two other things I should, of course, join with them in the verdict. Those points were: The identity of the body and that the child had died a violent death. Mr Dugdale, whose understanding of the law I accepted as a matter of course, said we must be satisfied about these two questions, and the judge himself had said if we were not satisfied we must acquit the prisoner.

A flurry of letters descended on to editors' desks from other jury members all damning George Euston and his stand. Some were hostile, others questioning, but none in agreement. Conscious of the debate being held in the press, the courts finally decided that it would be unwise, and possibly prejudicial to the case, were it to be reheard at the Spring Assizes. They did not agree with the editorial in the *Warwick and Warwickshire Advertiser* that demanded Elizabeth Brandish be given, 'the benefit of the doubt', and released. The retrial was set for July.

Mr Justice Darling took his seat at 10 a.m. on 28 July before another packed courtroom. Public interest in the trial had not waned with time and just as in March huge crowds swamped the courthouse. For three days they flocked to Warwick and the fortunate few sat enraptured by the witness accounts and the eloquence of Hugo Young's closing speech. Gone was the pretence that Elizabeth Brandish had given the child away and in its place the notion that the child in the garden of Drybank Farm could indeed have been Rees Brandish. But, as the articulate defence barrister verbally sifted the evidence, the question was, had the body found shown any proven signs of murder having been committed upon it?

The judge had absolutely no doubt it had. In his summing up to the jury he all but told them they must return a verdict of guilty. But they disagreed and after an hour and a half deliberating in the jury room returned a verdict of not guilty. Uproar met the foreman's announcement. The judge, no doubt incensed by the decision, ignored court protocol and did not tell Elizabeth Brandish that she was free but simply rose and left the court. Abuse was hurled by the crowds in the public gallery and a sense of astonishment shared by almost all in the courtroom, but Nurse Brandish had won the day.

Did she do it? Most probably she did. The body at the farm had to have been her son's. She was clearly seen and identified boarding the train at Towcester with him in tow. John Days the railway guard knew her by sight; he had seen her on several occasions and was adamant she and Rees were still together on the train at Blakesley. From there she had around fifty minutes before the train arrived in Ettington and when she left the compartment the little boy was not with her. At that juncture he had to be dead. She then had two options: one, she placed the little boy's body inside the tin bonnet box and carried it off the train and two, she ran out of time so wrapped the body inside her mackintosh. This along with the empty bonnet box she then carried from the train to the waiting room.

The author tends to favour this second scenario. When the porter, Hooten, barged in looking for his ticket, perhaps he unwittingly interrupted her as she was about to place the body inside the tin box. But by his own admission he did not linger, which still gave her time to complete the job. She then stepped out on to the platform, handed over her ticket and at the same time asked him to carry the box up to Drybank Farm, as heaving 2½st about would not have been easy. She was probably irritated by his refusal, but having visited Ettington so often would have known Heritage's parcel delivery routine and so found the bench, sat down and waited for him. The fact she refused the porter's offer of delivering her bonnet box the next morning is possibly significant. If it were true that her son's body was inside then it is more than likely she intended to bury him in her brother's garden that same night. If she had meant to take it with her to Clent the following morning, allowing the porter to deliver would have been perfectly reasonable.

In court unfortunately no measurements were ever given for this tin box. A bonnet box was so common, like a shoebox today, that a description was sufficient. But Dr

Holy Trinity and Thomas of Canterbury Church, Ettington. The broken headstones in the left foreground are the graves of Elizabeth Brandish's brother and his wife. (Author's Collection)

Fenton had no doubt it was perfectly possible for the boy to have been placed inside, and when Elizabeth arrived at the farm she had no bulky package, only the brown paper parcel Sarah Urben had given her back in Kent. There was nowhere else that the body could have been concealed. When she entered that farmhouse the little boy had to have been placed inside the box. That also explains the foetal position in which he was found. Once at the farm, of course, all she had to do was bury him in the early hours of the morning.

Circumstantial evidence says most definitely that she murdered him, but absolute and certain medical evidence was found wanting. Perhaps that was why the jury acted as it did. Or were they acting on purely altruistic grounds when they returned the 'not guilty' verdict? Two key factors ought to have influenced their deliberations. First that there could have been no doubt over the identity of the body found in the garden and secondly that there could have been no doubt as to who placed it there. Irrefutable, but it made little difference. Elizabeth Brandish appears never to have spoken publicly about her trial and died in 1927.

7

A DEADLY ENGAGEMENT

Baddesley Ensor, 1902

Born in 1874 at Hyson Green in Nottingham, George Place had never known any industry other than mining. Many of his family worked down the mines where conditions were poor but wages good. When he left school there was little doubt he would follow the tradition and so he did. By the age of 21 he had moved to Mansfield, still a collier, where he stayed for some years. During 1900 he made the decision to move out of Nottinghamshire and made the long trek west to the small mining village of Baddesley Ensor in Warwickshire. Why he decided to take work at the nearby colliery is not known but at about the same time he made the move he met Eliza Chetwynd.

Baddesley Ensor today viewed from the top of Boot Hill. (Author's Collection)

She was then a vivacious 18-year-old living with her family in a small cottage in Black Swan Yard off Watling Street. Place became a regular visitor to the house from the moment he arrived in the village. Totally besotted by her, he first began eating his meals there each evening when his shifts allowed and by the summer of 1901 they were lovers. Money had always been tight for the Chetwynds and as the relationship developed he suggested that for the sake of respectability he ought to move in, as a lodger, though it is doubtful he ever slept alone. The house had only one bedroom, which he paid rent for; her parents slept in the downstairs parlour, her younger brother Joseph slept on a settle in the kitchen, while her elder brother Jesse had use of a small box room. But his contribution to the household finances was no doubt gratefully received.

In January 1902, perhaps not unexpectedly, Eliza announced that she was almost two months' pregnant. Place, by now secretary to the local branch of Druids, which had brought him considerable respectability, immediately offered to marry her. There was no argument from the family and the wedding date was fixed for Easter that year. Unfortunately tragedy was to strike before their vows could be exchanged. Eliza's father died suddenly the week after the banns had been read in the local church. Their marriage plans were suddenly thrown into turmoil and there was no alternative but to cancel the ceremony in light of the unexpected bereavement and replace it with a funeral. What happened after that is a little unclear but it seems that Place was in no rush to rearrange the wedding. As a result of his wavering, relationships all round became understandably strained, but more so with his intended mother-in-law. The two had never seen eye to eye but for almost a year they had managed to share the same space without exchanging harsh words. That changed the moment she realised her daughter's future was in jeopardy.

On 14 August Eliza gave birth to a baby boy. Believing the child's father would never accept his responsibilities, and was more likely to run away than stay, her mother advised her to take out an affiliation summons against Place. It was in effect a bastardy order that when ratified by the court would acknowledge him as father and force him to pay maintenance for his son's upkeep. She did the organising and the summons was served six days later. Place was incensed and almost rigid with anger when he realised what she had done. Insisting to Eliza's brothers that there had been no reason to go to law in order to force him to pay, he reiterated his intention to be married. In a show of defiance he threw the order into the fireplace and watched it burn, telling the two men that he would have his revenge. Storming out of the house he left the village and went to his sister's home in Liverpool.

Place stayed away for three days and returned to the Chetwynds' on the Saturday evening. At 9.30 that night he walked into the nearby Red Lion pub and asked his drinking friend, John Radford, if he would loan him £6 so that he could pay Eliza to cover the cost of her confinement. Radford was not in a position to hand over such a large sum of money and told him so. During the conversation that followed Place told him if there was no money to be had he would resolve matters differently. From

The Red Lion Inn, Baddesley Ensor. (Author's Collection)

his jacket pocket he produced a revolver and made a clear threat as to what he intended to use it for: 'This will settle the job . . . they have got to die.'

A shocked Radford rebuked him and tried to seize the gun. Place refused to release his grip and said he would kill them all at six in the morning, and then left abruptly. Apart from discussing the strange encounter with a friend at the bar Radford did nothing. Certain in his belief that George Place was not a killer he convinced himself that it had been bluster from an angry man and went home to his bed. He was very wrong.

After a sleepless night, at 6 a.m. on 24 August 1902, Place calmly walked downstairs and entered the parlour. In the bed Eliza, her mother and the newborn baby were all asleep. Placing the revolver against the head of each in turn he shot them. Jesse and Joseph Chetwynd, Eliza's two brothers, found him outside the kitchen with the smoking gun still in his hand. He told them what he had done. 'It's all done and it's all over. I told them I would pay them, and I have paid them now.'

Offering the still-loaded gun to Joseph he asked him to take it and shoot him there and then. Joseph needed no second invitation and made a move to do exactly that, at which point Place panicked. The look of anger in the brother's eye was enough to convince him that retribution would be swifter than expected. Quickly he changed his mind, grabbed the weapon back then ran out into the street. Neighbour Joseph Shilton, who had been brought from his bed by all the noise caught up with Place on the Atherstone road and disarmed him. He was handed over to police and later that morning charged with murder.

Unfortunately for Eliza when Place left the bedroom she was still alive. The last of the three to be shot, she had obviously been awakened by the sound of the first two gunshots, and in a desperate attempt to save her life had made a grab for the gun. Grasping at the barrel of the weapon had deflected the shot, which had still hit her in the head but had not caused the type of extensive damage suffered by her mother and son. Medically, though, there was nothing that could be done to save her life. The bullet had penetrated too deeply, but she clung on as long as she could in a state of semi-consciousness, and finally died around mid-morning.

Place showed no remorse for his actions. According to Police Sergeant Flockton who made the initial arrest, he was cool, calm and collected throughout the proceedings. Neither did he offer up any excuses. Murder had clearly been his aim from the moment he left the bar of the Red Lion and he had stayed with his timetable: six in the morning had been the perfect time to kill – enough daylight to see by and all his victims asleep. In fact everything about his actions that morning had been planned, including his arrest. Place had never intended to go on the run, though he did tell police that he had considered drowning himself in the canal.

The inquest opened on Tuesday 26 August before north Warwickshire coroner Dr Iliffe. Given the option of attending or staying in his prison cell Place chose the

St Nicholas's Church, Baddesley Ensor, where the triple funeral took place. (Author's Collection)

latter, fearful of his reception by the gathering crowd, which was probably a sensible decision although the hearing itself was short, only taking identification evidence and the results of a post-mortem. These confirmed what was already known, namely that the killings had been carried out execution-style. The court declared Place guilty of murder and adjourned.

The triple funeral took place at Baddesley Ensor's parish church the next day in the late afternoon. Such was the interest that had been aroused by the local press that a crowd in excess of 10,000 people swamped the village and surrounded the graveyard. Eliza was buried with her 11-day-old son and all three shared the same grave. For all those who attended it proved an extremely heart-rending and cruelly emotional day. For the Chetwynd family, who had been devastated by four deaths in the space of five months, it was tragedy on a massive scale.

The trial opened on 8 December before Lord Chief Justice, Lord Alverstone. Place, a short, thickset man, took his place in the dock at 11.30 a.m. and after pleading not guilty was allowed to sit. There his interest appeared to wane and he gave the impression throughout the morning of being detached from the events going on around him. Not that it mattered greatly to the defence team, who had decided that the only avenue available to them was a plea of insanity. Price's seemingly callous indifference in court would have perhaps appeared to support their contention that he was mad, though they would need affirmation from a strong medical quarter if they were to convince the jury, and unfortunately for the defendant that was sadly lacking.

Cape Road prison, Warwick, where George Place was incarcerated. (Warwickshire County Record Office, CR2902/84)

The Chetwynd family graves. (Author's Collection)

After hearing witness evidence of the murder, and the events following, the medical men took the stand. Over the course of two hours the defence team attempted to show that at the time of the killings George Place was suffering from homicidal mania. They claimed he did not realise what he was doing when he entered the parlour and fired off three shots. Dr Power, who had examined the baby and the murdered women after the killings, agreed that it was a reasonable assumption to have made. Place, he told the court, had been involved in a roof fall at a colliery some years earlier and had suffered head injuries as a result. Those injuries could have caused a mental imbalance: 'Many cases of homicidal mania were of that character. A blow on the head many years before might be a cause of such madness.' He went on to explain in more detail exactly what this type of medical breakdown could do. For a while it looked hopeful, but then Warwick prison's doctor, Hubert Tibbits, was brought into court and he shared no belief in Place's mental decline.

According to his testimony, since Place's admittance into Warwick gaol he had exhibited no signs of insanity and after long observation appeared perfectly sane. The doctor went on to explain at length that his prisoner had thoroughly understood the nature of the charge against him and had at no time given any cause for concern over his mental capability. Despite rigorous cross-questioning he never faltered in his conviction that Place knew exactly what he had done and had not suffered a mental breakdown at any juncture of his life.

It was devastating for the defence and they knew it, but Horace Rowlands, QC, who had built his whole defence strategy around the notion of insanity, refused to abandon the idea. In his closing speech to the jury he told them it was the only viable explanation for what happened in the cottage at Baddesley Ensor: 'If a man could not distinguish between right and wrong then whatever else might happen to him he should not be condemned to death. If the act was done without motive it was the act of a madman. . . . Could they suppose that an ordinary decent man would commit such a brutal act if he was in his sound mind?'

In his summing up the judge was dismissive of this as an argument. He told the jury that no evidence had been produced in court that would support the belief that George Place had ever demonstrated to those around him a preponderance to insanity:

The man was assumed to be in his right mind unless there was evidence to show that he was not, that was to say, that he did not understand the difference between right and wrong. But it must be such a warping of the mind, such an unhinging of the mind, that he did not understand the difference, and the jury were not entitled to come to that conclusion unless they were satisfied that that was really his condition.

The jurors agreed and George Place was pronounced guilty after a few minutes' deliberation. He was executed at Warwick by Henry Pierrepoint at 8 a.m. on 30 December 1902.

8

THE BICYCLE LAMP MURDERS

Coventry, 1906

David Shell had been delivering bread to Hawthorne Cottage for four years. In fact he had probably been among the first locals to welcome Richard Phillips to the house after his marriage to Mary back in September 1904. It was the kind of home he aspired to own one day. Detached, double-fronted, fruit trees around the front door, extensive gardens on all sides, and all its boundaries surrounded by an attractive wrought-iron fence. If wealth were measured by the type of property a couple owned then, to David's mind, this couple had done very well over the years. It was probably a fair assumption to have made.

The view towards Stoke Park today. Hawthorne Cottage is thought to be one of the houses on the left. (Author's Collection)

Richard had spent all his working life in the watch-making industry where he had gained a reputation for quality among those that knew him. His decision to marry at the grand old age of 76 had come as no surprise to anyone, particularly when his bride, at 69, was even wealthier than himself. David had known Mary ever since her husband had died some six years earlier, and he knew that the house he so admired only looked as it did because she had lavished a deal of money on it over the years; she also owned the land opposite, which she had refused to sell as building land because it would have spoiled the view. So intent was she on maintaining the house the way she had always known it that cost had never been a consideration.

Yet money had never made her aloof or pretentious, so when David walked around to the back of the house on 12 January 1906 he anticipated his usual warm welcome. If he were lucky that welcome would also bring a cup of tea. But when he climbed the steps to the back door there was little to indicate that he was expected. The house was still in darkness, the curtains remained closed, and no lights were burning. He knew before he rattled the doorknocker that he was unlikely to be warming his hands by the kitchen fire, which he registered as odd. Mrs Phillips had ordered the delivery of bread, just as she had hundreds of times before. She had never forgotten. He knew if she had been called away she would have left a note. So he knocked again and as he waited he noticed something else that was unusual. There were a number of plates and bits of fruit scattered about the garden borders. The more he looked the more he saw. As he stood on the doorstep staring out at all this misplaced household crockery he thought it bizarre. But in his mind it made no other significant impact. Odd behaviour was the province of the old. So, after he had made a note in his delivery book to return the following day, he left.

The date of 13 January was a Saturday and David was intent on finishing early if he could. He arrived back at Hawthorne Cottage at around 3.30 p.m., this time seeking to deliver his bread as quickly as possible so he could be on his way. But when he rounded the corner at the back of the house he saw that nothing had changed. The house was still as it had been twenty-four hours earlier. The discarded plates and bits of fruit had not been retrieved, nor had anyone switched on any lights or bothered to leave him a note. Suddenly he felt a sense of unease. Unlike the day before when he had been prepared to accept what he saw as eccentric, the thought occurred to him now that perhaps it indicated something far more sinister. As he walked around the back garden he pondered that what he saw scattered around its borders had not been deliberately placed for effect but thrown out from the house. Then he noticed the open pantry window and it all made sense.

When Charles Chowler opened his back door minutes later it was to an excited, and by then much animated, delivery lad. For Chowler it marked the end of what had been a long, boring Saturday afternoon at home. So he was easily persuaded that there was something untoward going on at one of his neighbours. After listening to all David had to say he readily suggested the two of them force a way into the house to check the old couple were all right. David agreed and minutes later, after squeezing through the open pantry window, the two of them were inside

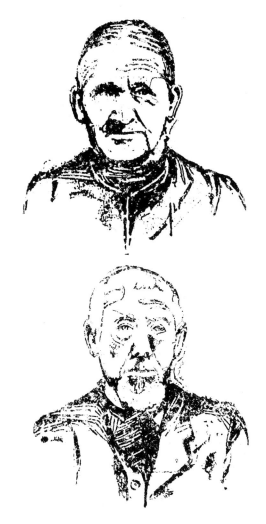

Drawings of the two victims and Hawthorne Cottage as it looked in January 1906.
(Midland Daily Telegraph)

Hawthorne Cottage. In the downstairs rooms they found no signs of disturbance. But as they reached the short landing at the top of the stairs the body of Mary Phillips was clearly visible through the open door to the main bedroom. She was sitting upright on the floor at the bottom of the bed, her right arm wrapped around the bottom half of the bedstead, her legs stretched out in front of her, and her head resting on her left shoulder. Blood had pooled all around her body, and splatter stains covered the walls and part of the ceiling. There seemed little doubt to the two men that she had been battered to death. Beyond her laid her husband, Richard. Face down, he was dressed only in his shirt, his head and shoulders partly under the bed, and most of his body covered in blankets that appeared to have fallen on top of him during the attack. He too had been savagely beaten. Beside him lay a closed penknife and in the corner of the room lay an open and empty cash box. Horrified at what they saw, both men fled.

Coventry's Chief Inspector Imber and his assistant Detective Sergeant Bassett were at the house within the hour. Clues were initially difficult to discover. Whoever had carried out the murders had left little behind and there was no sign of a murder weapon. But the calendar on the mantelshelf was still open at 10 January, which suggested the couple had been dead perhaps three days. Police surgeon, John Loudon, agreed. He carried out a reasonably thorough on-site examination of the bodies, which revealed enough evidence to support the theory that death had occurred thirty-six or more hours earlier. He also confirmed that in all probability Mary Phillips had been first bludgeoned while standing at the bottom of the bed, the blood splashes across the ceiling being clear indicators that she had been upright when she received the first blows, though death had not taken place until she had been beaten to the ground, probably as she attempted to reach the door. In Loudon's initial assessment he also told police that an undergarment found wrapped around her head had covered her mouth, possibly as a gag to keep her quiet as she died. In all, he counted six substantial blows about her head and added that he believed it likely the murder weapon had been a heavy chisel or a burglar's jemmy.

The same weapon had also killed Richard Phillips. Bloodstaining to the soles of both his feet, according to Dr Loudon, confirmed his had been the second death. The staining had been caused by him standing in his wife's blood as it pooled around her body and his injuries, sixteen substantial head wounds, were clear indicators that he had sustained the worst of the attack, though neither body had any defensive wounds to the hands or arms, which seemed to imply that they never saw the attack coming.

From the outset it was presumed that the motive for the double murder was robbery. The open cash tin was obviously proof that money had been taken, though no evidence was found to suggest exactly how much. Nightfall put an end to any meaningful search of the house and its gardens, though not the door-to-door enquiries, which went on until the early hours. They resumed again at dawn when new teams of officers arrived to carry out a search of the grounds. Information gathered from neighbours eventually confirmed the calendar date of Wednesday 10 January as being accurate. No one had seen the couple after their lights went out at around half-past ten that night. A further search of the garden revealed nothing new. So by the end of Sunday the investigation team were satisfied the killer had entered the house in the early hours of Thursday morning. This became an accepted fact after the milkman had been questioned. He was able to confirm that the plates in the garden had been there later that morning but had not been there twenty-four hours earlier.

By the end of Monday 15 January police told the waiting press they were satisfied that entry had been through the pantry window, which had clearly been forced, and that the motive for the murders had been money. None had been found in the house, neither had Richard Phillips's pocket watch, which he had always been known to wear. According to their initial statements nothing else appeared to be missing. It later transpired, however, that something had been left behind.

As a matter of routine Chief Inspector Imber had organised an inventory to be taken of all household goods. This enabled police to identify known possessions while at the same time ascertain any missing items. When the exercise had been concluded and losses identified they discovered to their surprise that the house had gained a bicycle lamp. Discovered on top of the mangle in the kitchen, it had been reasonably assumed to have belonged to the murdered couple. But the Phillipses had no bicycles and their children were able to confirm that the lamp did not belong to either of them. It was a key breakthrough; in his hurry to escape the killer had obviously become careless.

On 22 January a full description of the lamp was released to the press in the hope that someone would either recognise it or associate it with its owner. The *Midland Daily Telegraph* ran it alongside a photograph:

Small common plated oil cycle lamp, having been crudely black enamelled over, bottom slightly dented, green glass one side, red glass the other. The sidelights of the lamp have been covered over inside with thick paper fixed on glass with a cement or glue that resists heat. Oil holder slides out on lifting red glass up and is slightly loose. On the back of the lamp, which fits to a bracket, is the figure of a man with a cross on the front and holding a lamp extended. Name of the lamp is 'Mars' and is made by Albert Frank, German manufacturer. The wick of the lamp is similar to that supplied by ironmongers for paraffin lamps, and has a single black thread running through the middle.

Meanwhile, uniformed police were given the task of finding the shop that sold it and the name of the individual who bought it. This in turn led them to a stolen bicycle.

In September 1903 a young man, John Lamont, had reported his bicycle as stolen after he had left it outside the Star public house in Coventry. The police report had been filed and the bike had never been recovered. But after the publication of the lamp's description police received information that the lamp had been a part of this stolen bicycle. Furthermore they were told exactly where the bicycle was. They arrived at the door of a man named Harry Lester on 21 February. There the bike was found in a back shed, obviously minus the lamp. Lester told the officers that he had purchased the cycle legitimately but not complete. It then transpired that he had bought the wheels for 7s 6d from local man, Charles Taylor, and the frame from another local, Walter Eales.

When police arrived at Walter Eales's home he was able to tell them that he had purchased the frame himself from Taylor for 1s 6d with the intention of building himself a bicycle. He had subsequently sold it on only after he had discovered that Taylor had sold a pair of wheels that fit the frame to Lester. As he told police, there was no point holding on to the frame if Lester had the matching wheels.

Charles Ernest Robert Taylor was known to Coventry police as a petty thief; he had a court appearance pending for house breaking and theft, but he also ran his own business operating as a carpenter out of a workshop on Jenner Street in

Jenner Street as it looks today. (Author's Collection)

Coventry. The business, which had built up a reputation for quality over the years, probably derived in part from his father because he had taught his son all the necessary carpentry skills. Larceny had been a recent addition to his skill base, probably due to his business suffering a severe cashflow problem. Once the investigation descended upon his business this single factor influenced how he was viewed by the investigation team.

Taylor denied any involvement in either the killings or the stealing of the Lamont bicycle, but after police had searched his workshop this denial was met with total disbelief. Among the tools of his trade they discovered a quantity of black enamel, the type used to create a 'japanning' effect often used on bicycles and which had definitely been used on the cycle lamp. They also found paper of a type that matched that discovered inside the oil lamp and pieces of paraffin wick; the importance of this latter discovery was considered by the murder squad a vital and key piece of evidence. It had been noted that the wick inside the lamp had not been the type of wick normally associated with the lamp they had found. It was of a different make and slightly wider, so threading it into the lamp was difficult to achieve. For Taylor to have matching pieces was extremely damning. When his mother Ellen almost fainted after being shown the lamp taken from the Phillips's house, police charged him with murder.

Then Eales's brother, Thomas, came forward and told police that he had made two long chisels for Taylor just after Christmas, both of hexagonal steel and had altered the design of one just before the murders, turning up the end of one chisel to change it into what could be used as a jemmy or short crowbar. Taylor had paid 3s for the work. The other straight chisel he had shortened and Taylor had eventually returned it to him because it was no longer needed. Circumstantially this gave the young carpenter both the means to enter Hawthorne Cottage and the instrument to carry out the double murder.

In his final post-mortem report police surgeon John Loudon reiterated his original assessment of the murder weapon and expressed a near certain opinion that something akin to this type of crowbar had caused the injuries he had found. In fact he had gone so far as to carry out a series of tests with one bought locally to try and assess the type of wound it inflicted. These he had then compared with those sustained by Mary and Richard Phillips. It had proved inconclusive but had shown with a reasonable degree of accuracy that he had been correct in his assumption that the murder weapon had been of hexagonal design. In the police's mind, therefore, was sufficient justification for presuming the chisel Thomas Eales had made into a crowbar had been the murder weapon. It was a view reinforced when, after an abortive and exhaustive search of Taylor's house and workshop revealed nothing, Taylor himself refused to answer any questions as to its whereabouts.

On 10 March he made his first short appearance in court and was remanded into custody at the police's request for two weeks. They needed time to construct their case. While everything they knew of Taylor – his associations with certain members of the criminal fraternity, and his apparent involvement with the stolen cycle – seemed to suggest his involvement, they had no firm evidence to show he was a double murderer. All his clothing had been sent to Birmingham for forensic testing but none had revealed bloodstaining. A thorough search of his workshop and his parents' home, where he had been living, had also drawn a blank: no watch, no money, and no murder weapon. Investigations into his movements on the night of the killings were also inconclusive. Though his whereabouts that night were relatively easy to prove up to a point, no one could testify to having seen him after around 11 p.m. and he was not willing to talk. All the evidence was purely circumstantial. Police were satisfied he had stolen the Lamont bicycle, retained the lamp after selling the various parts on, had the necessary paint and paper to have made the alterations that made the lamp so distinctive, and had certainly owned the means to allow him to force an entry into a house. But after a further two weeks of investigation they had discovered nothing else.

On 24 March, smartly dressed in what the *Midland Daily Telegraph* described as 'a lounge suit of rusty black', he stepped into the dock of the Coventry City Police Court at half-past ten in the morning. Every seat had been taken and the court officials were forced to find extra seating for the huge numbers of people that had queued for entry since well before nine o'clock. This was the court that would hear all the evidence and decide whether or not Taylor should stand trial at the later Assizes. To some extent it was a foregone conclusion. Despite the police's inability to discover any significant evidence that would tie Taylor irrevocably to the crime, enough existed to cast a long shadow of suspicion across his life. He had, at this juncture, still refused to reveal the whereabouts of the crowbar. He had also continued to deny selling on bicycle parts that were undeniably those from the Lamont bicycle and, perhaps more damning, had refused to accept that the cycle lamp had ever been in his workshop. Whether circumstantial or not these key facts left the court little room for manoeuvre and Taylor was inevitably sent to trial.

It opened on 23 July before the Hon. Bernard Seymour, Lord Coleridge, KC, commissioner of Assize. Prosecution counsel, with a history of success in murder cases, was Henry Yorke Stanger and for the defence Henry Joy. For Taylor of course this was his last chance for life. Unlike the hearing back in March, if he lost this case there would be no appeal and he would make the short walk to the gallows. This was a trial for high stakes. During the preceding three months or so he had continued his denials, and maintained throughout that he had not murdered the Phillipses in their own home. For the defence this would have been expected and was no doubt seen as laudable, but they also knew that innocence was likely to be difficult to prove. When the prosecuting counsel sat down after a two-hour summation of the Crown's case the outlook must have seemed somewhat bleak.

The remainder of the first day was spent hearing evidence from neighbours of the deceased and those who visited the house between 10 January and when the couple's bodies were discovered on the 13th. The intention was to create a timeline of events that established their movements, as far as was possible, and set an approximate time of death. But it was the second day of the trial that caused the first sensation and for the defence the first serious blow to their case.

While Taylor had been incarcerated in Warwick prison police had certainly not been idle. A combination of publicity and door-to-door enquiries had produced a key witness. Haulier John Boneham had come forward to say that on the morning of 11 January he had reason to go to Kenilworth railway station, but before he could set out he had to call at his stables, in a field off Walgrave Road. There was a footpath that ran from this field to Binley Road, yards from Hawthorne Cottage. At between 4.20 and 4.30 a.m. he saw a man exit an alley at the bottom of this path, walking towards Coventry. The two passed each other, no more than 2ft apart, and the haulier wished him 'Good morning.' From the witness stand he told the court that the man wore an overcoat with the collar turned up and was carrying something, which he could not see, but because the night was clear and moonlit he had no difficulty in seeing the man's face. At a later police identity line-up he had pointed out Charles Taylor. It was the first piece of evidence that placed Taylor near to the scene of the murders and at about the right time.

Boneham was followed to the stand by Taylor's mother, who confirmed that her son had not slept at home on the night of the murders. In mitigation of this she added that he had slept in his workshop after drinking too heavily, though she was unable to offer any evidence to support that notion other than what her son had told her. But this was quite possibly true. During the investigation police had unearthed enough witnesses to corroborate the fact that he had consumed a fair amount of

Binley Road as it looks today.
(Author's Collection)

alcohol on the night of the killings. It was therefore reasonable to presume he may have chosen to stay in the carpentry shop rather than go home. What time he arrived at the workshop was the debatable point. Ellen Taylor realised this was a key point and tried hard to add to information that would help fill in the gaps: 'I asked him why he had not come home as usual and he replied, "I broke the pledge yesterday and was ashamed to wake you up." He said he had spent the night in the shed [workshop] in Jenner Street. He said he came to the back and there was no light, and he went to the shop. I think it was between eleven and twelve. If he had come to the front I would have heard him.'

She went on to tell the jury that his clothes showed no signs of bloodstaining, and they were the same ones she had seen him wearing the day before. Under rigorous questioning from both sides in the courtroom she denied her son had any other clothing other than that which had been seized by police. This, of course, was a blow to the prosecution who knew full well that whosoever wielded the murder weapon would have been covered in blood. If it had been Taylor, as they believed, then he had to have been able to change his clothes and possibly destroy those worn during the attack. But Ellen Taylor was immovable. She was equally so when it came to identifying the cycle lamp. She told the court that her initial belief when she had first been shown it by Chief Inspector Imber had been wrong. She told the jury that police officers had been in and out of her house on nine separate occasions prior to the murder, seeking evidence to assist them in an earlier prosecution for theft. She had become weary of questions and had therefore mistakenly believed that the lamp she had been asked to identify was the same as one she had seen previously. But, she now insisted, she had been mistaken and the lamp produced in court was not the one her son had once owned. That lamp she had not seen for over a year.

Ellen Taylor: I have seen a lamp at home which was like the one produced. It was the fact that my son's lamp had red and green lights.
Judge: Your son had a bicycle lamp?
Ellen Taylor: Yes, my Lord.
Judge: It was kept on a tall shelf in the scullery?
Ellen Taylor: Yes, my Lord.
Judge: Have you ever seen that lamp since 11 January?
Ellen Taylor: No, my Lord.
Judge: When did you last see it?
Ellen Taylor: A week prior to Whitsuntide 1905, when we had the decorators in.

Despite further questioning from both the judge and the prosecution counsel she would not be moved. It was the first hole in the police case. What they had hoped was that Ellen Taylor would be forced to admit that the lamp found had been the one she had seen in her own home. So the scene was set for the final day.

When the judge took his seat before a packed courtroom at ten the next day the case was finely balanced. The prosecution had successfully placed Taylor at the scene of the crime in the early hours of the morning of the murder. The defence on the other hand had cast sufficient doubt over the cycle lamp ever being in his possession, which in turn called into question the accuracy of this identification evidence. So the jury verdict at that juncture must also have been impossible to judge.

When the prosecution counsel opened the final day of the trial they knew that if they were to prove guilt, they must show how Taylor succeeded in hiding the crucial evidence that would convict him. The murder weapon was out of their hands. There was nothing they could do that would produce it in court. If a police search over several weeks had failed to locate it then it was never likely to appear before the case concluded. What was needed was a way of demonstrating how the second most crucial piece of evidence, the clothing worn by the murderer, had disappeared. Ellen Taylor's testimony in defence of her son had cast doubt on the amount of clothing her son had owned, but it had not dispelled it. The prosecution knew that whoever carried out the murders could not have left Hawthorne Cottage without being bloodstained. The jury were about to hear hard evidence in support of that theory.

From the witness stand police surgeon John Loudon reprised his post-mortem examination report and told the court that both Mary Phillips, and her husband, had almost certainly been struck while standing, though not at the same time. His supposition was that the elderly couple must have been in bed when they heard the intruder. Mary Phillips was the first to get up and was struck as she reached the end of the bed. Her husband must have witnessed the attack and gone to her aid. Of the six blows to her head one had severed a major artery, with the result that blood would have spurted upwards and backwards as her head moved under the blows. So much blood was lost during the attack on Mary that it pooled all across the bedroom floor. With regard to the gag placed around her mouth, Loudon told the judge, he could not state with certainty that it had been placed there either before or after she had been hit, but the evidence tended to support his earlier supposition that it had been done as she lay dying. In the case of her husband, he had sustained sixteen distinct blows across his face and head and had been pushed beneath the bed after he had died.

At that point the full horror of the murder was brought home to everyone in the courtroom and an understandable hush fell across all present. So brutal and frenzied was the attack that there could be absolutely no doubt that whoever carried it out could not have walked away without blood splashes across most of their outer clothing, and the prosecution was certain that the man responsible was Charles Taylor.

After hearing the devastating effect of the attack upon the old couple and being shown photographs of the scene, the jury now clearly saw the significance behind the prosecution assertion that Taylor had destroyed his clothing before police found him. But with no corroborating evidence discovered, and the examination of clothing seized by police revealing absolutely nothing, it was left to the Crown to demonstrate the veracity behind their theory.

Charles Taylor took the stand at a little after 11 a.m. After the defence had established his background and allowed him the opportunity to reaffirm his movements on the night of the murder the prosecution was given its opportunity. A ripple of excitement swept the public gallery as the erudite figure of Henry Stanger rose to his feet.

Over the three days of the trial it had been established that Taylor had all his suits made. What had not been clearly established was just how many he possessed and Taylor was extremely evasive when questioned.

Stanger:	I think you said that the clothes you were wearing on the 10th of January were what the police afterwards had?
Taylor:	Yes, that is a fact.
Stanger:	What other suit had you then?
Taylor:	As I have told you, only one, this one.
Stanger:	Do you mind telling me again?
Taylor:	Yes, certainly, this one.
Stanger:	Were those the only two suits you had at this date?
Taylor:	The only two suits I have worn the last eighteen months.
Stanger:	I want to know the number of suits you had?
Taylor:	Well, the police say they found one old suit.
Judge:	Answer that question. How many suits had you on the 10th of January.
Taylor:	Three.

The number of suits established, Stanger then began to assert that only two had ever been found. The obvious question was, what happened to the third? Taylor told the court that the three had been made over a period of some two years and that one of them had been cast aside at some point owing to too much wear and that he had a habit of giving away his old suits. It may not have been a satisfactory answer but was certainly one that would have been better understood then than it would be today. Ready-made clothing was not easily available, and it was the tendency of most people to eventually use older clothing for work. Denim was a thing of the future.

Having established that Taylor had possessed more clothing than had been found, the prosecution had sown the seeds of doubt. But when it came to demonstrating their belief that Taylor had burnt the clothes he had worn when he had entered the Phillips' house they were less successful. Nothing Taylor said from the witness box contradicted his mother and his insistence that after sleeping in the workshop he had returned home in the same clothes was difficult in the extreme to disprove. Added to this was the fact that the police search of his premises had revealed absolutely nothing, no fragments of burnt clothing, no odd buttons, nothing in the ashes of a fire. In short, nothing that supported the assertion he had done as they believed. He left the witness box after three and a quarter hours, his defence still intact.

In his summing up to the jury the judge was extremely forthright when he told them that the case was one built upon evidence that was all purely circumstantial. Nothing had been produced in court, he told them, that would amount to a confession. Nothing had been produced that would prove conclusively that Charles Taylor had been in Hawthorne Cottage and no eyewitness had been discovered that saw him either enter or exit the house. But enough evidence existed to link him to the killings. He outlined the evidence of the cycle lamp, the black enamel paint found in his workshop that had possibly been used to paint it. The brown paper used to cover one of the lights, the fact that he had certainly handled and sold a stolen bicycle from which the lamp had been taken, and lastly the fact that he had not returned home on the night of the murder. When the jury retired, the case was still as finely balanced as when it began. It was no surprise when they returned a verdict of 'Not Guilty'.

For Charles Taylor the verdict was not the end of his involvement with the police. The pending court appearance for theft outstanding at the time of his arrest for murder saw him back in court weeks after this acquittal. Found guilty of housebreaking and the theft of a quantity of farthings he was sentenced to eight years in prison. He was released in 1914. After joining up at the outbreak of the First World War he was invalided home in 1917 suffering from shell-shock and spent some months in Hatton Asylum. On 9 April 1922 he committed suicide in what can only be described as extremely bizarre circumstances. He was found hanging from a tree on Gibbet Hill, Kenilworth, at the exact location of the old gibbet.

Was he guilty of the murders? The circumstances of his suicide would suggest that he was, though no firm evidence of blame was ever produced. If he did it there can be no doubt he suffered greatly from his guilty conscience, and little wonder. He and his father made the coffins in which Mary and Richard Phillips were buried. They also laid out the bodies and it was his own father who subsequently carried out the funeral.

9
THE PRICE OF HERRING

Leamington, 1907

Fanny Moore and her husband Edward had lived in Leamington just about all their lives. Married in the mid-1880s they had successfully brought up six children, despite the cramped conditions of their small terraced house on Oxford Street. Money, of course, had always been in short supply, as it was for all those who lived around them. Having only one wage earner in the house brought its inevitable pressures, notwithstanding this they had never fallen into poverty. Edward was well respected throughout the town and reasonably well known through his work as a local cabman. This had meant that over the years the family income, while modest in comparison to some of their neighbours, had not suffered as a result of the fluctuating fortunes of local industry in which the vagaries of the market place dictated both wage levels and employment, something Edward had been able to avoid.

The Parade at Leamington, c. 1900. (Author's Collection)

Oxford Street, Leamington, today. (Author's Collection)

By the start of 1907 only two of their children remained living at home: Bertie, who as an 11-year-old, as well as being the last addition to the family, was too young to go out to work, and 33-year-old Edwin. In the latter's case unemployment had never been an issue but the ability to hold down a job for any length of time had. Edwin had been a problem to the family for much of his adult life, though as a young man expectations had been high. An extremely successful gymnast in his youth, he had won numerous accolades from his trainers for dedication to the sport, which he had translated into competition trophies and a much-vaunted medal given to him by Queen Victoria.

But all the high hopes and optimism dissipated as soon as he reached his 20s. Unable to realise any of those earlier aspirations and possibly very keen to escape Leamington, he enlisted in the 1st Battalion, Warwickshire Infantry Regiment, in the mid-1890s. After basic training he was sent to India. Here he suffered a severe bout of sunstroke, the result of which brought him back to Britain and a dissolute lifestyle. The relationship with his parents inevitably suffered. He was arrested on nine separate occasions for being drunk and disorderly and in 1904 he was finally imprisoned for three months after being found guilty of theft. When he returned home the gulf between him and his parents had widened even further. Edwin's increasing dependency on drink resulted in more frequent rows and during one explosive argument towards the end of 1906 he cornered his father in the attic and threatened to hack him to death with a meat cleaver. From that point on the two men found it impossible to be in each other's company.

On Saturday 2 March 1907 the by now extremely volatile Edwin spent the afternoon at a local football match. On his return home he called at the Stoneleigh Arms for several drinks and arrived home at about 7 p.m. His father was still out at work. Supper was to have been fish; his mother had cooked herring earlier in the evening, which she had kept hot on a low heat in the oven. Unfortunately, Edwin was no fan of fish, and no sooner had he walked in through the back door than he began to rage at the strong smell, which permeated the whole house. Fanny had learned over the years that it was best to ignore his tub-thumping and, working on the principle that if he were hungry he would eat, she served the fish at the kitchen table despite his protests. But Edwin refused to be placated by the sight of food irrespective of its smell. Instead he threw the hot plate into the air and kicked it at the wall before it hit the ground. Food debris along with broken crockery were scattered across the kitchen walls and floor.

Fanny had never seen this sudden irrational behaviour before and recognised all too late that she was in danger. As she ran for the door Edwin grabbed the lit oil lamp from its place on the table and hurled it at her. She managed to duck away before it smashed into the wall. Oil splattered across the walls, door and floor but did not ignite; only the wick continued to burn. But Edwin was not prepared to allow his mother to escape. Taking an old newspaper from a chair in the kitchen he hurriedly rolled it into a long paper spill, dipped its end into the burning wick then grabbed her by the arm. After a brief struggle she broke away and ran into the long hallway between the kitchen and the front door of the house, but he caught her before she was able to get outside. Callously, he then simply thrust the burning newspaper at her then stood back to watch. Her blouse ignited instantly, seconds later the flames were around her head, fire caught hold of her hair, and as she ran screaming back towards the kitchen scullery she was alight from head to foot. Edwin slowly followed her, careful to stub out the burning newspaper on the kitchen table.

Bertie, the younger brother who was sitting by the kitchen window when Edwin arrived home, had witnessed everything that happened. As his mother tried desperately to douse the flames around her it was he who ran out into the street screaming for help. Greengrocer James Phillips whose shop was opposite the house was first on the scene. In response to the boy's frantic shouts he managed to burst through the front door within seconds of Fanny reaching the kitchen. But here his way was suddenly blocked. Edwin, indifferent to his mother's distress and still full of anger, met him in the burning doorway between kitchen and hallway. He refused Phillips entry, swore loudly at him, then by way of reinforcement used his fists to knock the grocer to the ground. As he stood triumphantly over the prone figure the fire behind him suddenly seized hold of the back of the house. Flames from his mother ignited the scullery's wooden shelving; fire then spread rapidly towards the oil spilled earlier and within a short time the kitchen floor, doors and table were well alight. Edwin realised all too late just what he had done. Neighbours poured into the hallway desperate to reach his mother and douse the fire that threatened their own homes. This time he offered no resistance and after removing his jacket ran to help.

Fanny was dragged out into the yard, wrapped in floor matting and rolled along the ground until all the flames had been smothered – but she was already dead.

When local police in the shape of Sergeant Rainbow arrived at the house Fanny was lying in the back yard. The fire was out but she was still smouldering from the waist up. Edwin, with his hands badly burnt, stood over the water butt by the yard's back wall. At that stage everyone believed Fanny's death had been caused accidentally, Edwin was not going to disillusion any of them by incriminating himself. He told the sergeant there had been some sort of explosion and that he had not been in the house when it happened but had been outside in the yard. When he found his mother she was desperately trying to douse the flames about her head in the scullery sink. He insisted he had done all he could to help her and had suffered severe burns as a result. Holding out his hands, the policeman could see they were bleeding badly, and in places had lost a lot of the skin around the palms, which seemed to corroborate Edwin's account. Certainly at that stage the policeman believed him and so organised transport to get him to the nearby Warneford hospital.

Later that same evening Detective Sergeant Matthews, who had been told that the death was accidental, arrived at the hospital to take a statement. Edwin did not deviate from the account he had given hours earlier. Adamant he had not seen the fire start, only its results, he continued the lie that his mother's death had been caused by some sort of explosion: 'I had just had a herring and went into the back, when I heard an explosion and saw flames in the house. I ran in and found my mother was on fire. I tried to put the flames out and put some water on her. . . .' As he went on to describe how neighbours had run to help and how his hands had become so badly burnt because he used them to beat out the fire, his account became ever more convincing. Unfortunately for Edwin other members of the police were already piecing together a totally different version of events based upon the evidence left in the house and, in particular, from young Bertie.

A thorough examination of the kitchen later that same evening revealed a number of anomalies in his account that were at odds with the evidence. Nothing had been found to prove an explosion, and the fire had clearly started in the hallway not in the kitchen. A rolled-up newspaper had been discarded with only one end burnt away, and oil from the lamp had been found on the walls. To add to all this the remains of the evening's meal were scattered all around the kitchen and the oil lamp, smashed apart, lay in pieces all over the kitchen floor, with the largest patch of oil splashed around the doorway leading into the narrow hall passage. It became clear to the investigating officers that the herring had never been eaten and the lamp had been thrown across the room with some force. At that point the credibility of Edwin Moore's statement was called into question. Bertie, in an interview later that same night, then destroyed it utterly. Edwin was formally charged with murder the following day.

The trial opened nine days later, on 11 March 1907. In the interim Edwin had refused to change his statement. Bertie therefore, became the focus of the day. In order to save the defendant from the gallows it was crucial that his version of events was shown to be untrue. He was the witness those packed into the courtroom had come to see. When the

The courthouse at Warwick.
(Author's Collection)

11-year-old took the stand at the end of the morning session a nervous silence fell across the court. Prosecution barrister Mr J.J. Parfitt quietly asked him to tell the jurors exactly what he had seen almost two weeks earlier. In a clear voice he described in some detail the argument his elder brother had caused, how he and his mother had shouted at each other from opposite sides of the kitchen, and how Edwin had smashed the dinner plate before grabbing the oil lamp:

> Edwin took up the lamp with his left hand and swung it round at mother. I could not say quite exactly where it hit, but it did not hit mother. She just dodged the lamp . . . it went crash against the wall . . . it [the wick] fell on the floor near the leg of the table, and was burning. . . . He [Edwin] took the *Evening Mail* off the table, screwed it up, and lit it from the wick. . . . Edwin came with the lighted paper, and near the door he took hold of mother's right hand and was holding this lighted paper to her blouse. . . . It flared all up. . . .

Powerful and horrific, the story's impact on the jury was devastating and, the more Bertie told the court, the more damaged became the defence's case. So, in a lengthy cross-examination the defence lawyers attempted to minimise its effect by trying to show that the evidence he had given was seriously flawed. Their contention was that the boy's story was not a true version of events. The lamp-throwing incident they did not contest. Evidence provided by the police had been compelling enough despite Edwin's continued denial. It was the deliberate setting alight of the evening newspaper they wanted to disprove, or at the very least cast doubt over it. Here the defence argued strongly that the newspaper had caught fire accidentally and that Edwin had stubbed it out before his mother was set alight. But Bertie refused to budge. He disagreed with the defence assertion that he had not witnessed his own brother commit murder and, seemingly undeterred by the hostile questioning, continued to maintain that he had seen the whole episode from start to finish. For Edwin it was the end. He must have realised as he stood silently in the dock that there was only ever going to be one verdict.

When the court adjourned for lunch there was one final opportunity to amend his earlier statement in favour of one that at least offered the court a mitigating reason for his actions, but he refused it. When the afternoon session began his version of events was read out to the court by Leamington's chief constable, Thomas Earnshaw. Clearly at odds with his brother Bertie's testimony, and in part already disproved by the evidence of the two policemen called to the house after the fire, it did nothing to further his defence. But, in his closing speech to the court defence barrister, Mr J.B. Marshall, continued to insist that Fanny Moore's death, while tragic, had been accidental:

> Within an hour of the affair the prisoner told the story of it being an accident and this was the story he had stuck to ever since, and he contended it was the true one. The man made desperate efforts to save his mother, and in doing so burnt his hands badly. If, in the deliberate and brutal way suggested, he of malice aforethought intended to kill his mother, was not this a most extraordinary revulsion of feeling within a very short time?

The judge, Mr Justice Phillimore, did not share a similar sentiment. In his summing up he told the jury that if they accepted that Edwin had exhibited anger prior to throwing the lamp at his mother, then it was a case of murder: 'No doubt after the offence there came a natural revulsion, and the prisoner endeavoured to undo the mischief, they [the jury] would hope for his mother as well as for his own neck. But it was none the less murder. There was no halfway house here. There was no suggestion of manslaughter. It is murder or nothing.' The jury agreed and after an adjournment of thirty minutes returned the expected verdict.

The execution date was set for Easter, Tuesday 2 April. For the remainder of his imprisonment Edwin received no visits from his immediate family, neither did his father attempt to obtain a reprieve for his son. So devastating had the murder been that he had found it impossible to intercede on his behalf. This in turn had lessened the impact of the plea for clemency made by his defence and it was quickly rejected. Perhaps understanding his family's reluctance to help, Edwin wrote to his father. It was a very poignant and extremely sad letter in which he accepted his guilt but made no confession.

He was hanged the following day at Warwick by executioner John Ellis.

10
A GRUDGE KILLING

When Harry Parker married the love of his life in the summer of 1902 he earnestly hoped, and believed, that his life would change for the better. Initially it did; like most newly-weds, married life began as a huge, enjoyable adventure. But as the love affair cooled so the adventure was replaced with normal routines and mundane demands. These same routines soon placed a strain on the marriage, which both found difficult to cope with. Within a few months of exchanging their vows the relationship began to break down. One year on, as the couple celebrated their first wedding anniversary, the marriage was in serious trouble. Harry, by this time, had found it hard to hold down a job. Financial restraints had caused local industries to adopt a less than liberal approach when it came to recruitment. With no permanent work available, Harry had been in and out of work throughout much of that year. Inevitably money had been in short supply. In turn their debts grew, tempers flared, arguments became a daily occurrence and the reasons for being married evaporated.

Stoney Stanton Road today. (Author's Collection)

By the spring of 1904 his wife had left him. Desperate to maintain her independence she had taken lodgings in Coventry, then found herself work at Meads Bakery, Stoney Stanton Road. A devastated Harry, who at that stage had no idea where she had gone, refused to accept the relationship was at an end. Within a few weeks a little rudimentary detective work had discovered the lodging house. Skulking around on street corners until he could follow her to work he eventually found the bakery. At that point the opportunity for reconciliation was his if he wanted to take it. But then, seized by a sudden fear that her leaving had been about more than just arguments and money, he backed off. Instead, he purposely stayed in the shadows, preferring to watch her from a distance, convinced that in doing so he would discover the real reason for their break-up. Jealousy had persuaded him that there was more to the bakery than just making bread.

This sense of mistrust was foolish and irrational but to Harry it seemed a logical train of thought. Why else leave a perfectly good marriage? In his mind he saw Thomas Meads as a wealthy man: a bakery owner, a local businessman, someone with enough money to buy whatever he wished for, someone attracted to his wife. The reasoning may have been spurious but to Harry there was an irrefutable logic. Several days' observation from a safe distance was enough to convince him the logic was sound, even though he had not witnessed any impropriety. All he ever saw was his wife arriving at work early and leaving late. But to his suspicious mind all those late shifts simply added to his sense doubts about his wife's trustworthiness. So, in a sense, the more he observed the more he believed he saw infidelity. His thought process was illogical but Harry had ceased all rational thought the minute he left home. Determined to put an end to what he earnestly believed was a burgeoning affair he made the decision to confront Meads at the earliest opportunity.

The two men met in the autumn of 1904 when Parker finally stepped out of the shadows one dark evening and accosted the baker as he left his shop. There was an argument of sorts in which he accused Meads of harbouring his wife and keeping her away from the marital home. A brief scuffle ensued, which ended with a beaten Harry forced to resort to hurling a few stones and a handful of dirt as he retreated. All this was witnessed by chief baker, Tom Hopkins, but the incident ended before he could intervene. However, Meads, not a man to meddle with, was not about to let matters rest there. He had Hopkins fetch the police and then insisted that a summons be issued for assault. Harry was later arrested, hauled up in front of a magistrate and fined 5s he could ill afford. Incensed by what he believed had been an injustice perpetrated by a rich man he left court determined on revenge at any cost.

What no one could have anticipated was that it would take as long as it did. On 26 August 1908, four years after the incident outside Meads bakery, Harry was back. During the intervening years there had been no reconciliation with his wife. She had eventually moved on from the bakery to employment elsewhere. But his sense of deep-seated anger over his treatment by the court and the circumstances surrounding his prosecution had never diminished. For Harry it was payback time. The year 1907 had been yet another bad one and he blamed this on the two bakers,

Thomas Meads and Tom Hopkins; Meads over the episode with his wife, and Hopkins because it had been he who had brought the police to his door after the altercation outside the bakery. This was a completely illogical train of thought but inexplicably one Harry had no difficulty in accepting. Desperate, short of money, out of work and seething with unresolved anger he arrived on Stoney Stanton Road in the middle of the night.

After sleeping out in nearby woodland he was outside the building at half-past four in the morning. Still familiar with the normal workings of a bakery, he knew that Hopkins would be opening up at about 5 a.m. He also knew he would be alone when he arrived. With a lighted pipe for company he hid himself behind a wall and waited. Ever the punctual baker, Hopkins was predictably on time. Harry, unarmed, stepped forward as he made to open the front doors. Despite the distance of years the old baker recognised him immediately but sensed no threat. The two men exchanged pleasantries for a few minutes then Hopkins, believing Harry would just go about his business, turned his back while he finished unlocking the doors. It proved to be a fatal mistake.

Harry waited until the baker went inside. When he knew he could not be seen he reached down, picked up a length of timber from among a pile of bricks, and stepped in behind him. Without warning he struck Hopkins a killing blow to the back of the head. The baker was dying by the time he hit the ground. Impaled by a single nail protruding from the club end of the wood, the base of his skull had been shattered. Blood sprayed across the floor until Tom Hopkins stopped moving.

Horrified at the sight of the stricken man, Harry panicked. All thoughts of hunting down Thomas Meads suddenly evaporated, to be replaced with the more urgent need to be elsewhere. He ran some distance from the bakery but then forced himself to stop, suddenly realising he ought not to be seen fleeing the scene of a murder. In an attempt at nonchalance he struck a match, hunched over the flame and carefully relit his pipe. He then slowly made his way to his mother's house. Unfortunately his timing caught him out. Harry had already been seen. Timber haulier James Gray, who knew him by sight, was on his way to work as the match flared. Recognising Harry, he spoke to him as he passed. Harry of course ignored him and turned his head away but the damage had been done. The body was found an hour and a half later and he was the only suspect.

Arrested within hours of the discovery Harry made no attempt to either deny his involvement or mitigate his actions. When eventually interviewed by Coventry's Detective Sergeant Cox he remained calm and extremely rational, explaining how he had spent the previous night outdoors, then with an unexpected candour told of how the killing had been done: 'He turned round to go to the bakehouse, and I hit him on the head. He fell down near the line post and I left him on the ground and went away . . . having no work I felt wild and went there to quarrel with him, and I hit him instead. . . . I knew I hurt him, as he lay pretty still while I was there.'

After the inquest, which declared Harry guilty of wilful murder, he amended this statement slightly. In the press the murder made headlines, which brought notoriety

The old police station at Coventry, now part of the council house.
(Author's Collection)

to his name in a way he had neither planned nor expected. As he languished in prison he then appeared to take solace from his fame, however fleeting, and he wanted more. When brought up before the magistrate's court he was desperate to give the crime a greater impact and so expanded his initial statement: 'It was a bad job I did not do them both and make a clean job of it.'

It was a moment of pure madness. Up until that point, despite his admission of guilt, there was every possibility that the court would have accepted a manslaughter charge. Admitting that it had been a premeditated murder, which is exactly what this additional comment implied, was damning in the extreme. Sent for trial at the Assize court the verdict was essentially one of formality.

The trial itself began on 26 November 1908 in front of Mr Justice Sutton. Harry Parker appeared strangely confident throughout and for much of the proceedings sat in the dock with an expression of amusement on his face. But there was little to be amused about; as the trial wore on his cause faded with the daylight. Defence barrister, Mr Sandlands, QC, had been severely handicapped by the confession and Harry's later comment, but attempted to show the court that murder had never been the intention.

After hearing from a variety of witnesses he contended that none had been able to show that Harry Parker had ever threatened murder, nor had he ever discussed revenge. In his closing speech to the jury he told them that had Parker intended to kill when he went to see Tom Hopkins then he would have carried a weapon. Not to

The narrow lane leading to Cuckoo Lane where public executions were once held. The building on the left is the gaol in which Harry Parker was imprisoned.
(Author's Collection)

do so meant that he had never intended the outcome that he caused. Striking the deadly blow, argued the QC, was an impulse action. The result of that same action was accidental death. Pointedly he asked the jury, how could Parker have known there was a nail protruding from the wood he picked up and how could have known, therefore, that the blow he struck would be deadly?

> There was no adequate motive for the crime. It was only a fancied grievance, even if it were a grievance at all. . . . No reasonable man could expect that a blow from such a piece of wood would have been attended with so fatal a result. If there had been no protruding nail just at that particular point there would have been no serious consequence. It was an accident that there was a nail there at all. . . . He went there to pick a quarrel, it was true, but not to kill.

It was a valiant attempt to deflect the jury from the charge of murder and had not Parker sought to enhance his criminal prowess for the benefit of the press it may have worked. As it was the judge lessened the defence counsel's impact when, during his summing up, he told them that when they considered the evidence of premeditation they had to consider Harry Parker's own admission.

He was found guilty after an adjournment of 1 hour and 40 minutes and executed at Warwick on Tuesday 15 December 1908. On this occasion John Ellis, who had executed Edwin Moore the year before, acted as assistant to Henry Pierrepoint.

11

A MARRIAGE MADE IN HELL

Harbury, 1922

When Rosilla Patience Borton, known as Rose, married her lover in February 1918 at Harbury parish church she believed they were perfectly matched. It had been a whirlwind courtship – the two had only known each other for about twelve months – but she felt certain that their relationship would only strengthen as the years passed. Life, it seemed to her, had turned full circle. Two years earlier she had stood in the same church but under cruelly different circumstances. Then, after the unexpected death of her young husband, she had found herself widowed at the age of 18 and the service had been one of remembrance. With his untimely death

Harbury parish church. (Author's Collection)

had come not only great sadness but also financial hardship. Understandably Rose's view of life at that point was somewhat jaundiced, but with help she had endured. Twenty-four months later pessimism had been banished and for a second time in her short life she had become the radiant bride once again.

However, the man who shared her marriage vows, William Rider, was wholly undeserving of the affection she had showered on him. At 36 years old when he walked down the aisle, he had a well-earned reputation as a womaniser, with a somewhat unsavoury past. He had two illegitimate children, which Rose knew of, and had lived a somewhat promiscuous lifestyle for too many years to change overnight. He was also still married, something neither Rose nor any of her family were aware of, and he intended it to stay that way.

The couple moved into a house in Pennington Street, Rugby, a home they shared with his two children, and almost from the minute Rose set foot inside the house their relationship changed. A violent man and a bully, he began to attack his new wife with his fists within days of the wedding. Over the next three years these assaults grew ever more frequent, with Rose taking a battering whenever he felt angry, drunk, upset, neglected or ignored, which meant she was never far away from a beating. On five separate occasions she ran back to her mother's house in Harbury where she would shelter for a few days. But Rider was nothing if not persuasive when it came to women and every time she fled she returned after he uttered a few conciliatory words. Always penitent towards her after any violent outburst, this act of contrition was all it needed to convince her that his violence was unintentional and she always made her way back to the marital home.

Pennington Street, Rugby, today. (Author's Collection)

In the summer of 1921 Rose's mother, Rachel Freeman, desperate to find a way for her daughter to leave Rugby and return to her permanently, was told about Rider's double life. Gossip, spread about the village throughout June of that year, had speculated on the validity of Rider's marriage after he had apparently been recognised by a man who knew him from some years earlier. According to this unnamed man Rider had married some years before he had met Rose and this first wife was still very much alive. By July these rumours had been substantiated by others who were able to confirm that not only was she alive and well but that he had never divorced her. Neighbours rushed to Rachel Freeman's door with the news. She in turn sent her 15-year-old daughter Winifred off to Rugby to pass the information on to her sister and awaited what she believed would be the inevitable outcome. But Rider surprised her yet again.

When Rose confronted her husband with what had now become common knowledge he did not deny it. Instead he told her that he had been misunderstood and that whatever had once existed between himself and his first wife was long dead. So convincing was he in his assertion that it had been the earlier marriage that had been the sham, not the current one, that she actually believed him. So did Winifred. The 15-year-old, who had always been attracted to Rider, possibly needed less persuasion than her sister. When she realised the couple were not going to split up as a result of the message she had brought, not only was she relieved but she also asked to stay. Rider readily agreed, unabashed by her obvious attraction, and all too eager to take advantage of her vulnerability given time and opportunity. He would be given both in the months that followed.

Winifred stayed with them for the whole of the next year. Totally besotted by Rider she refused to return to Harbury despite her mother's pleading, choosing instead to stay as close to him as she could in the hope that her feelings would at some stage be reciprocated – and of course they were. A sexual predator like Rider was never likely to allow a chance for seduction to pass him by. They became lovers behind Rose's back. All would probably have been well had they practised some form of safe sex. There is no evidence to show that she ever discovered their secret relationship but almost certainly Rose harboured her own suspicions. Rows became more frequent through the early part of 1922 and all of them centred around her young sister. Rose, who the previous year had agreed to allow Winifred to live with them, now wanted her sent home. Only Rider's intransigence kept her at the house and that in itself added to Rose's sense of misgiving. But matters were about to take a dramatic turn. By the end of July Winifred had discovered that she was pregnant. Forced to tell her mother, who caught the first available train to Rugby, she was hauled off back to Harbury and Rider was reported to the police by a mother intent on revenge. The marriage was suddenly at an end.

By the middle of August 1922 Rose had moved out of the house in Rugby and was back living with her mother at Binswood End, Harbury, though she had still not severed all ties with Rider. On 26 August he sent her a message and asked that she meet him in Leamington and she readily agreed. Rider failed to keep the

Binswood End as it looks today. (Author's Collection)

appointment and when Rose got back to her mother's house Winifred was found to have gone missing. It transpired later that the meeting had been mere subterfuge. Rider had already prearranged with Winifred that they meet at Leamington railway station. The two then disappeared together for some ten days, travelling between Banbury and Shrewsbury, staying in hotels along the way. Rachel Freeman went back to the police demanding that they do something.

During the early evening of 6 September an unrepentant Winifred finally arrived back home alone. Fiercely loyal to Rider she refused to acknowledge that the pair had been together since her disappearance, despite her mother's insistence to the contrary. The denial cut no ice with her sister either and the row that followed was as protracted as it was noisy. Winifred was eventually forced to acquiesce to the two women's view that if nothing else her behaviour had been irresponsible. Still defiant, she was then sent to bed. But the damage had already been done and Rose knew it. She sensed that Rider was unlikely to leave Winifred alone, particularly after spending time on the road with her. Frightened by the prospect of him arriving at the house during the night and what would happen if he did, she made her mother make the property as secure as she could, but it was never going to be enough.

At 10.15 p.m. Rider knocked on the door of the Harbury police house. Convinced that a police search had been mounted while he and Winifred had been travelling around the country, and that a warrant of some kind had been issued for his arrest, he had decided it was prudent to surrender himself to the village constable. But the police had been tardy. No one had searched for him, no manhunt had been mounted and the constable had gone off on holiday. So, dismayed at the lack of interest and after a brief conversation with Mary West who slept at the police house, he went back into the village.

At 7.10 the following morning, after a night sleeping rough, he succeeded in forcing a downstairs window at the house on Binswood End. Once inside he took off his boots and climbed the stairs. Only Winifred slept alone, Rose, her mother and youngest sister, 13-year-old Minnie, all shared a bedroom at the back of the house. Of the three only Rose had a bed to herself and her bed was directly opposite the door. All too well aware of the family's sleeping arrangements, Rider knew exactly where to find her. Slowly he eased the bedroom door open and stepped inside. As he did so something in his movements disturbed Rose. Suddenly aware of someone framed in the doorway she sat up. Recognition was instant, as was the fact that he carried a shotgun. All she had time to shout was, 'Oh, Bill don't.' She took the full blast in the left side of her head and was killed instantly.

A scuffle followed as her mother ran across the room and attempted to disarm him. Desperate to prevent him reloading she pushed the barrel up towards the ceiling and tried to wrest it from his grasp while daughter Minnie ran for help. But he was too strong. The two of them fought a frantic battle beside Rose's bed until Rider, who actually had no intention of killing again, shouted at her that if she did not release the gun he would throw all his remaining ammunition on the downstairs fire and blow the house up. Believing the threat to be real she let go. Still holding on to the gun, he then turned and fled but was grabbed on the stairs by Arthur Large and his wife Edith, near neighbours who had run in to help. A second brief scuffle ensued, during which he admitted killing Rose, before he managed to force his way past and out into the street.

From the house he ran to a ramshackle, disused outhouse building some 40yds away from its back door. There, he returned the gun to its earlier hiding place along with all the remaining cartridges and made off towards Leamington where he was arrested later that same morning outside Whitnash golf course, though not initially for murder. Police sergeant George Grooby, who made the arrest, knew nothing of the shooting when he made what was effectively no more than a routine check. If Rider had not looked so dishevelled after his night outdoors, the policeman would probably never have given him a second look. Unfortunately William Rider was not to know that. He believed that news of the murder had travelled ahead of him and he was now a wanted man. So, before the sergeant was able to ask questions, Rider confessed to the killing, although careful to add that it had been unintentional: 'I accidentally shot my wife this morning in Harbury. I was coming to Leamington to give myself up.' At that point he was cautioned, advised to say no more, then taken to Leamington police station. From there, after some preliminary questioning, he was removed to Southam and later that same day charged with murder.

The inquest opened before mid-Warwickshire coroner E.F. Hadow at the Dog Inn, Harbury, thirty-six hours later. William Rider, who had insisted on attending, was brought to the makeshift coroner's court handcuffed to a policeman. Hundreds had turned out to watch his arrival and the crowd inevitably swamped the inn long before the court proceedings began, with every available vantage point being taken. After hearing evidence of identity the morning's first witness was Rose's mother. She recounted the events that had led up to Rose leaving the marital home, gave details of

Rider's intolerable behaviour towards her daughter and described some of the violent episodes that had peppered their marriage. She then explained how she had discovered some weeks earlier that this same marriage had been a sham after it had come to light that Rider was a bigamist. Recalling the murder itself she was very precise as to how events had unfolded and rejected out of hand a suggestion by the coroner that it could have been an accident. Rider, she pointed out to the court, had taken off his boots so as not to be heard. He had intended to kill Rose, she insisted. Nothing about his actions suggested anything different and no one in the house knew of his presence until the gun was fired.

When Dr James Pirie stood in front of the court he appeared to support Rachel Freeman's contention that it had been murder. There was nothing in the nature of the wounds, he told the coroner's jury, to show the gun had not been carefully aimed. No shot had been deflected and almost every one of the 136 pellets he had fired at Rose had hit her in the head. Rider, he insisted, had stood no more than 1ft away from her when he had fired. In his opinion had the shot been accidental then the wound would probably not have been so extensive and a number of pellets would have more than likely missed their mark.

For Rider, who stood in silence listening as the evidence against him mounted, it must have been a somewhat sobering experience. Throughout the day he only ever saw one familiar face and that was Winifred's. When she took her place in court she refused to offer any testimony against him. A troublesome and recalcitrant witness, she was eventually led away in contempt of the court. But it made no difference to the coroner's outcome. The jury was unanimous in its 'guilty of wilful murder' verdict and he was returned to Southam in a sombre and reflective mood.

Headline of Rosilla Borton's murder.
(Warwickshire Advertiser and Leamington Gazette)

TERRIBLE TRAGEDY AT HARBURY.

YOUNG WOMAN SHOT DEAD.

RUGBY MAN IN CUSTODY.

The peacefulness of Harbury was rudely disturbed on Thursday morning by a terrible tragedy, as a result of which William Ryder, aged 40, is in custody on a charge of wilfully murdering a woman known as Rose Ryder, aged 21 years.

It appears that the couple, who had gone through a form of marriage, had lived at Rugby during the last five years, where Ryder worked as a chimney sweep and collector of rags and bones. It is stated that differences had arisen owing to the visits of the woman's sister Harriett, age 16 years. A week ago the dead woman returned to the home of her mother (a Mrs. Freeman) at Harbury, and it was arranged that she should go into domestic service at Gaydon yesterday.

On Wednesday evening Ryder appeared on the scene, and just after ten o'clock called at the Police Station, where he discovered that the village constable had gone away on his holiday. The constable's niece (Miss Plummer) and a friend were in, however, and from their bedroom window answered the man's enquiries. At first he wanted a glass of cold water as he had walked from Rugby and "had been on the booze." It should be stated that the police had been making enquiries respecting Ryder's relationship with the girl, and no doubt being under the impression that a warrant had been issued for his arrest on a criminal charge the man said he desired to give himself up. He was told that there was no constable in the house to whom he could surrender, and that the nearest police station was at Southam or Bishop's Itchington. He was told which way to go, but, curiously enough, he made off in an opposite direction. Other inhabitants state that Ryder called and asked for a glass of water.

What Ryder did during the night is not apparent, but he undoubtedly wandered about the lanes surrounding the village awaiting the time for the men to go to work.

At seven o'clock, it is stated, Ryder broke into Mrs. Freeman's house in Binswood End, and, after an altercation with Mrs. Freeman (who endeavoured to prevent him from being violent) dashed upstairs where Rose Ryder was in bed.

Pointing a sporting rifle at her, it is alleged that he pulled the trigger and the charge entered her head, killing her instantaneously. He left the gun in the room, and there being only women in the house Ryder took advantage of the ensuing confusion to leap through the window and escape. He was not to remain long a fugitive, however. P.C. Loach (Bishop's Itchington) on being informed of the crime, acted with commendable promptness. He got into communication with Inspector Scott, of Southam, and a description of the wanted man was circulated.

It fell to the lot of the Leamington Police to effect the man's arrest—and this was a smart piece of work. The Chief Constable (Mr. T. T. Earnshaw) was at breakfast when the message reached him at 8 o'clock, and he at once placed all his available officers to scout and watch the roads leading into Leamington. At best the description of the fugitive was a poor one, and practically all that could be ascertained was that he had a mark on his neck, and was known at the fried fish shop under the railway bridges.

At nine o'clock P.S. Grooby and P.C. Forest, who had been told to scout Whitnash district, saw a man hurrying along the cinder track by the railway not far from the golf links. The officers jumped off their bicycles and intercepted the man, who exclaimed, "I have shot a woman at Harbury, and I was just going to give myself up!"

He had the appearance of having been out all night, and his clothes were wet. The man, after being brought to the Leamington Police Station, was handed over to Inspector Scott.

The validity of Ryder's marriage is being questioned. It is stated that he had been previously married and had two children.

FARMERS AND THRESHING MACHINE CHARGES.

The conference between representatives of the National Farm...

The Dog Inn at Harbury,
where the inquest was held.
(Author's Collection)

Two days later the body of 24-year-old Rosilla Patience Borton was released to her family and the burial took place at Harbury. Almost all the village turned out as a mark of respect to watch the funeral cortège as it wound its way through the street. Most had known her, many were her friends, and those closest to her in life formed a long snaking procession following on behind the coffin. According to the *Warwickshire Advertiser and Leamington Gazette* a deal of anger was apparent among those in the crowd around the cemetery after the service; many were keen that William Rider be brought to book and none believed his plea of innocence. What had happened to Rose during her short marriage had not gone unnoticed. Most were all too well aware of just how badly she had been treated, and of Rider's reputation before he took the mock wedding vows four years earlier.

As for the man himself he had two weeks in which to concoct a defence that would be acceptable to the upcoming magistrates' hearing and remove the murder charge from his head. But he had no realistic defence. The only option available to him was to continue to insist that he had never intended to fire the shot. If he was to do that he must show that Rose's mother and her sister Minnie had either lied at the coroner's court or had been mistaken when they claimed to have witnessed the whole event. His contention was, as he took the stand on 25 September, that Rachel Freeman had lied. Through his defence team he told the court that she had struggled with him the moment he entered the room. The gun, he insisted, had then fired accidentally and Rose had been hit in the head as a result. If Rachel had not attacked him and made a grab for the gun it would never have fired and Rose would still have been alive. It was a completely unconvincing argument and one that was systematically destroyed by the prosecution as the day progressed. The magistrates readily convicted Rider of murder and sent him to the Assize courts to stand trial.

The case opened on 17 November at Warwick before Mr Justice Lush. It was a foregone conclusion. The same witnesses took the stand and without exception told

Southam, c. 1900, where William Rider was taken after his arrest. (Warwickshire County Record Office, PH350/2017)

the same story. Police had discovered that the gun had been purchased while Rider had been on the run with Winifred, which in turn implicated her in the murder, though she denied any knowledge of the purchase and claimed it must have been made when she was absent. How the gun was then transported back to Harbury unseen, she was unable to answer. At the end of a very long day the jury returned the expected guilty verdict and Rider was sentenced to death.

A petition was immediately launched to appeal on the grounds that the trial judge had misdirected the jury during his summing up,and had not allowed sufficient character witnesses for the defence. The Court of Criminal Appeal sat on 4 December to consider the argument. Two presiding judges, Justices Darling and Salter, heard the evidence ably presented by Mr Eaden, QC, on behalf of Rider and summarily dismissed it. The case, argued Mr Justice Darling, was simple enough: was it murder or was it an accident? If the latter then it had to be proven. He insisted that if a man had accidentally shot his wife would he then have threatened to blow up the house? Reading from the court testimony he then referred to the words Rider was alleged to have uttered after the killing: 'If you don't let go of the gun I will go downstairs and put cartridges on the fire and blow the house up.' Added to that, the judge went on, was the fact that immediately after fleeing the bedroom and being momentarily stopped by Arthur Large and his wife he had acknowledged his guilt: 'I did it in a fit of temper.'

The defence barrister had no argument persuasive enough to nullify those two key statements and, despite a valiant attempt to argue that Rachel Freeman had been mistaken in her testimony, the appeal was thrown out.

William Rider, 40, was finally executed by John Ellis at Birmingham prison on Tuesday 19 December 1922.

12

THE RADIO HAM

The society wedding of Arthur Crabtree and his new wife Milly in July 1923 had attracted its fair share of newspaper interest. Arthur was the son of a prominent Halifax town councillor, and highly regarded in business circles where he had gained an enviable reputation as a gentleman farmer and keen huntsman. Owner of Church Farm on the outskirts of Neston, Cheshire – where his agrarian skills had proved extremely successful and from where he had managed, through good breeding, to build a flourishing dairy herd – he was the archetypal eligible bachelor, handsome and very rich. For 22-year-old Milly he was the perfect match. Born in Bradford, she was the daughter of another well-known northern farming family, the Fawcetts, who owned an equally successful farm at Allerton. In terms of status, therefore, which mattered greatly to both families, their standing in society was near enough equal. So, when the pair exchanged their vows in St Mary's Church, Halifax, the bond they formed was both emotional and, without doubt, financial. Their first child, a son, was born in June 1924 and their second a year later.

The fickle nature of farming, however, means that success and failure are often unwelcome partners. In the early part of 1925 the Crabtrees had first-hand experience of this when they suffered two unexpected blows. First, the weather destroyed a large proportion of their arable crops and, second, the much-prized cattle were hit by foot and mouth disease. The farm took a significant financial hit, although not one they were unable to recover from as Arthur's wealth ensured they suffered no serious hardship; but one that triggered a change. The farm at Neston was suddenly placed on the market and sold by the summer of the same year. Intent on staying in farming Arthur then moved his family to Warwickshire in September and on the 29th of the month moved them into Manor Farm, Ladbroke.

The farmhouse at Ladbroke they shared with their stockman Sibert Coleman and his wife and daughter. The house was large enough to accommodate all and it obviously made sound business sense. Along with the two families came 19-year-old labourer George Sharpes. He had worked for Arthur Crabtree for some fifteen months and was keen to escape Cheshire. Born in Crewe he had spent four years in a reformatory school at Newton-le-

Ladbroke village, c. 1900. (Warwickshire County Record Office, PH352/107/14)

Willows after being caught breaking into a church when he was only 14, something he was desperate to leave behind him. He was equally keen that no one should know of this criminal past and he saw the move as an opportunity to make a fresh start. An introvert, his only interest outside his work was his radio. An avid fan of almost everything the BBC was able to offer, all his evenings were spent listening to various programmes. At Neston he earned 10s a week, lived at the farm and received his board and lodgings free. His needs were few and while the wage was low it mattered little to him so long as he could keep his radio running.

The Crabtrees of course knew his history well and what reservations they may have held initially had been dispelled by his attitude to work. Arthur liked him and certainly trusted him. Neither he nor his wife had any qualms about bringing him down to the new farm in Warwickshire, but they could not continue with him sharing their home. Once it had been decided that the Colemans would move into the house, its lack of a spare bedroom meant that George would have to take rooms elsewhere. Captain Wheeler, the farm's previous owner, pointed them in the direction of his carpenter at Rectory Farm. He was only too willing to take the young man in and after a brief negotiation a weekly rent of £1 was agreed. The Crabtrees then increased George's weekly wage to take account of his new circumstances and presumed all was well. They were wrong.

George moved down from Cheshire in early October and at first found things to his liking. But as the weeks passed he began to resent being excluded from the farm and its evening routines. While the 17s increase in wages that had been agreed ensured he could pay his rent, it had actually left him with less disposable income than at Neston. This meant saving was more difficult and it took longer to set aside the money needed to renew his radio licence. By Christmas he had also discovered that his criminal past had not been left behind as he had hoped but had travelled to Ladbroke with Milly Crabtree. Obviously not blessed with a deal of sensitivity when it came to discussing her employee's past failings, she had made it common knowledge in the village. George began to harbour sinister thoughts of revenge.

On Sunday 9 January 1926 Arthur returned to Cheshire to finalise the sale of Church Farm. There were papers to sign and an inventory to be agreed before the sale could be finally concluded. He left George under Sibert Coleman's control and told the family he would return before the end of the week. It had been agreed some days earlier that the inside of the house would be given a much needed lick of paint and so, during his absence, Milly coerced Sibert into releasing George from his normal afternoon routines. The walls had to be stripped of years of neglect and she and Arthur had agreed he was best equipped to do the work. Happy enough to be out of the cold George raised no objection and so each day after lunch he reported to the house and picked up a scraper. But being in such close proximity to the woman he blamed for all his ills was not the best place for George to be.

On Wednesday 13 January his sense of resentment finally got the better of him. In an act of sheer, unprovoked horror, he seized hold of a hammer and, in what he believed to be an act of retribution, struck Milly down with a single blow to the back of the head as she passed him in the hallway. She never saw her attacker and was almost dead when she hit the floor. With great presence of mind George then dragged her body into the sitting room where her 6-month-old baby sat crying on the settee. There he stayed for some fifteen minutes staring at the dying woman, unsure of what to do next. Milly was still breathing but every breath was a rasping struggle for air. George wanted to silence her, to stop the noise. He struck her a second blow with the hammer in the same spot but it had no effect. Desperate, he then walked out of the room in search of something with which to gag her.

In the hall the Colemans' 10-year-old daughter Kathleen suddenly stopped him short. Unbeknown to him she had been playing in the kitchen with the Crabtrees' other son and wanted to know if Milly was ready to feed the two children. He told her to go back and wait then ran off upstairs. He returned to the sitting room minutes later with a pair of pyjamas, which he wound tightly around Milly's head until her breathing had stopped: she was finally dead. It was half-past two in the afternoon and the baby had still not been fed. Inconsolable in its hunger it began to cry ever louder and George, as if awoken from a stupor, flew into a sudden panic. Leaving Milly where she lay he ran from the room and upstairs to the Crabtrees' bedroom where he laid on the bed and cut his own throat. Unfortunately for George his knife was blunt.

An hour later young Kathleen, concerned over the crying baby, wandered into the bedroom in search of Milly and found him still very much alive. George was conscious and bleeding heavily from the throat but still able to speak. From his prone position he told the little girl to go and find her father and bring him to the house. Kathleen needed no telling a second time. She could see from the amount of blood around his neck and the staining across the front of his shirt that he was badly hurt. Frightened by what she had seen and scared for the baby, she turned tail and ran.

Sibert Coleman found him minutes later. George, desperate to die but without the tools or the courage to finish himself off, was by this time full of remorse. For over an hour he had lain in his own blood staring up at the bedroom ceiling – ample time to reflect on the full horror of what he had done. Almost as an act of contrition he refused help and in a few whispered words confessed to murder. Sibert, somewhat taken aback by the sudden admission, was momentarily unsure how to react. But George had been unequivocal in his confession and that in itself convinced him of its truthfulness. He found Milly seconds later where she had been left on the floor of the sitting room, the carpets around her soaked by blood and on the settee her young baby crying for his dead mother.

Inspector Cresswell of Southam police arrived within half an hour of the farmer raising the alarm. Milly's body lay face down, her feet near the door and her head pointing towards the window, with the murder weapon, later described as a carpenter's hammer, on the floor in front of the sofa. Crucially Cresswell noted that blood had not only pooled around her upper torso but had also splashed across walls, windows and an oak bureau some 5ft away, a clear indicator that she had died in the room in which she had been found. Coleman then told him of George Sharpes's confession and took him upstairs to where he still lay bleeding on the bed. The inspector made a cursory examination of the man's wounds, which he quickly realised were not life threatening and decided to leave him where he was until a doctor could be found to carry out a more detailed examination.

William Lattey, Southam's surgeon, arrived a little after four in the afternoon. He concurred with the policeman's assessment of George's injuries and after applying a dressing to his throat organised for him to be taken to the Warneford hospital at Leamington. Inspector Cresswell added the precaution of a police guard. Lattey then proceeded to carry out a more meticulous inspection of Milly's wounds before her body was removed. This revealed that she had sustained a massive fracture to her lower skull just behind the left ear, caused he believed by the hammer found at the scene. A blow, he conjectured, that had been struck from behind and one that meant her death had been near instantaneous. To the inspector that appraisal of events supported Sibert Coleman's statement that George had admitted to murder when he had been found earlier in the afternoon. The young farm hand was duly charged with the crime later that same day.

The inquest opened at Ladbroke's village hall on Saturday 16 January. Milly's husband Arthur told the court of his marriage and their decision to move to Warwickshire. He went on to give an account of how he had first met George Sharpes and his decision to employ him despite his past criminal record. He insisted George had never exhibited any signs of being mentally unstable. But it was 10-year-old Kathleen Coleman who proved to be the most damning witness for the young farm labourer. She gave an account of the events leading up to Milly Crabtree's death and of how George had figured in them. Crucially she told the coroner that between two and two-thirty that afternoon she remembered that she had seen him come out of the sitting room twice. On the second occasion she recalled that he had blood on his hands and according to her testimony she had asked him why. He had told her that he had simply cut his fingers and was going to wash the blood away. But, according to Inspector Cresswell who followed her on to the stand, the blood had still been on his hands when found. He hypothesised that although George had attempted suicide with a knife the nature of his injuries suggested that it was reasonable to assume that most of the blood on his hands was not his own. Despite the obvious flaws in that argument the coroner accepted it as being a plausible assumption. The court returned the inevitable guilty verdict against George.

Hours later the funeral of Milly Crabtree took place at Ladbroke parish church. On a bitterly cold day, with several inches of snow on the ground, most of the village attended the graveside service alongside her family.

Just over one week later, on 25 January 1926, Sharpes stood in the dock of Southam's magistrates' court for a brief two-minute hearing before being remanded for a further week. At the resumption on the following Monday he was formally charged with murder and ordered to stand trial at the Spring Assizes. The murder trial opened on Tuesday 9 March before Mr Justice Shearman. Smartly dressed in a light grey suit, white shirt and black tie, Sharpes was four weeks away from his 20th

Ladbroke parish church today. (Author's Collection)

The grave of Milly Crabtree. (Author's Collection)

birthday when he entered the courtroom. After being advised to plead not guilty he took his seat in the dock, flanked by two warders, and watched in silence as proceedings got under way.

The cause was lost from the outset. There was no defence that would stand up to scrutiny and, of course, Sharpes had already admitted his guilt. His defence team took the only avenue available to them: insanity. But proving he was mentally incapable when he raised the hammer and struck the blow that killed Milly Crabtree was an impossible task. No doctor was prepared to offer any medical evidence in support of their case. Most damning of all was Hamblin Smith, Birmingham's prison doctor, who had had Sharpes under close observation for the previous four weeks. He told the court that despite the young man's poorly developed physique he had exhibited no signs of mental collapse, and nothing in his demeanour while in prison had suggested insanity at the time of the killing. It took the jury only thirty minutes to pronounce him guilty. An appeal was immediately launched to save him from the gallows, still along the lines of insanity but claiming that the trial judge had not fully explained the notion of insanity to the jury. Lord Chief Justice, Mr Justice Avery, and fellow judge, Mr Justice Finlay, disagreed. They threw out the appeal on 1 April. A second appeal, this time signed by 6,000 residents of Crewe, Sharpes's home town, was presented to the Home Secretary seven days later but with the same result.

Hangman William Willis executed George Sharpes at 8 a.m. on 13 April 1926 at Birmingham's Winson Green prison.

13

THE BOMBING OF
BROADGATE

Coventry, 1939

As the somewhat muted celebrations that had heralded the arrival of 1939 faded into memory the western world turned a cautious eye in the direction of Germany. There, under the leadership of Adolf Hitler, the Wehrmacht, a military force of some 1¼ million men, was poised to attack Poland. If and when they did every political leader across Europe knew a second world war would become inevitable. For the British government the desperate race to re-arm had already begun. Badgered and cajoled by Churchill they had been forced to recognise the growing military threat posed by Hitler's Nazi Party and were already actively preparing for what they believed would be an inevitable war. In so doing they perhaps understandably failed to recognise the lesser yet more immediate threat at their own back door.

In Northern Ireland the IRA, which had remained active since the Easter uprising, saw themselves not only as a militant resistance movement but also as the heirs of the original Irish Republic declared in 1916 and therefore the rightful rulers of all Ireland. In practice, of course, they represented the irreconcilable residue of Republican separatists who objected to the presence of British authority on any part of Irish soil, though no doubt a view they would not have agreed with and certainly not a view shared by their supporters. They were arguing vociferously that if there was to be an end to the partitioning of the north then the IRA had to change public opinion, and if that change was to be brought about by acts of violence then so be it. During November and December 1938 they began to put together a document intended to raise the profile of their cause. After Neville Chamberlain's return from Munich that same year clutching Hitler's paper promises in his hand the British public, apparently happy to be deceived, had turned their back on unpalatable truths. This the IRA probably saw as an opportunity and on 12 January 1939 they delivered their ultimatum to the Prime Minister and sent copies to the Governor of Northern Ireland, the German Führer and the Italian Duce, Mussolini: 'I have the honour to inform you that the government of the Irish Republic, having as its first duty towards the people, the establishment, and maintenance of peace and order, herewith demand the withdrawal of all British armed forces stationed in Ireland.'

Its implied threat was a violent one. The IRA were effectively giving notice that if the army did not withdraw, which they no doubt knew would not happen, then they would believe themselves justified in taking whatever action they deemed effective. Four days later, with the government refusing to acknowledge the IRA's demand, a series of bomb explosions took place in various locations across England. In London three blasts badly damaged electricity plants. In the north and in the Midlands further blasts damaged gas mains and in Manchester a 27 year old fish porter, Albert Ross, became the first terrorist victim when he was caught in an explosion on the outskirts of the city.

The IRA apologised for the death but did not stop planting bombs. In March they made a failed attempt to blow up Hammersmith Bridge, and in June again attacked the capital's utility installations on four separate occasions. On 26 July an Aberdonian doctor, Donald Campbell, became the country's second terrorist victim when a bomb planted in the left luggage department at King's Cross railway station exploded beside him; it also injured fourteen others. On the same day, and timed to coincide, a second blast at London's Victoria station wounded a further five. This brought the total number of terrorist outrages for 1939 in both the UK and Northern Ireland to 127, and some 57 of these had taken place in London. But people were finally waking up to a dual threat: that posed by the terrorists, who were clearly living among them, and that posed by the fascists who intended to live among them. They began to voice their concerns. Critics of the government were not slow to react either and there was a general unease among those who filled Parliament's debating chamber.

Two days later, in an attempt to stifle this criticism and restore confidence in the government's policy of non-appeasement, Home Secretary Douglas Hoare rose to his feet in front of a packed House of Commons. In a short speech he explained how, since the original bomb blasts in January, police had carried out a series of successful raids at homes around London. This had resulted in the arrest and conviction of 66 IRA members. The raids had also discovered 1,500 sticks of gelignite, 1,000 detonators, 2 tons of potassium chlorate and 7 gallons of sulphuric acid. He also announced a new Bill intended to allow the issuing of expulsion orders against any terrorist subject and widening police powers in order that they were able to prevent any character they believed to be suspicious entry into the UK. But for some this was all too late.

Against this backdrop of terror and increased police activity a young plasterer named James Richards arrived in Coventry and took lodgings on Meadow Street. Richards, whose real name was either McCormac or McCormick, was born in Tullamore, West Meath on 7 July 1910. Since leaving school in 1924 he had held several semi-skilled jobs but never managed to remain employed for long. Exactly when he had joined the IRA is not known but he was certainly a member by the time he arrived in England at the end of 1938. Initially operating out of a flat in Paddington, London, he made the move to Coventry in May 1939. His new landlords, fellow Irishman Joseph Hewitt and his wife Mary – neither of whom

Meadow Street, Coventry, as it looks today. (Author's Collection)

knew anything of his terrorist connections – readily accepted him into their home. They needed the extra money a lodger provided and Richards's Irish background suited the two of them ideally. With a 15-month-old baby to feed and clothe and an aged mother to look after, the additional income was much needed. Brigid O'Hara, the mother in question, was an overweight, garrulous woman, but her presence in the house was crucial. Had she not been there Mary would not have been able to take a job at a nearby shop, neither would Richards have been fed on time each day. However, there was a price for all this. Brigid had an inquisitive nature and an unfailing appetite for gossip, not a problem for the family but one Richards had to watch very carefully.

What the Hewitt family was totally unaware of was that their new lodger was an IRA courier. He travelled between London and Coventry on a regular basis, maintaining contact with terrorist cells in the south and carrying back potassium chlorate for use in bomb making. This he kept in a suitcase under his bed but as time went on he found it more and more difficult to conceal, so the Hewitt's decision to move to a larger house only a month or so after his arrival came at just the right time. He, along with all the family, moved to 25 Clara Street on 12 June. His frequent journeys to the capital continued, as did the arrival of new suitcases at the Coventry address. This in turn began to arouse suspicion, particularly from Brigid, but Richards convinced her that he was simply taking care of clothing for friends. As an excuse he knew it would be accepted for a while but not in the long term. He therefore set about trying to find a safer, more inaccessible place in which to keep his bomb-making chemicals. The cupboard under the stairs was his first choice. Unused by anyone else in the house and, with a dirt floor beneath the floorboards, it was ideal. So, when the house was empty he set about lifting the floor and digging a hole.

Unfortunately for Richards, what he had not foreseen was the attention of nosy neighbours. Clara Street was a short street of brick villas in a built-up area of Coventry. Considered by many to be a good middle-class residential part of the city, it meant that when people made changes it was noticed. So when Richards was seen carrying rubble out into the garden it was Mary Hewitt whom the neighbours questioned. Unaware of her lodger's secret dig, but all too well aware of the government's new stance on suspected terrorists, Mary suddenly felt herself to be under some sort of suspicion.

Newspaper reports over the previous few weeks had been dominated by IRA activities in London. She, her family, and in particular her lodger, were all Irish, which, as she was all too acutely aware, made her vulnerable to all sorts of conjecture without having a tenant that dug up the floor while she was at work. After making up some excuse about internal alterations she went home to her husband, suspicions aroused, and demanded that he throw Richards out. But Joseph Hewitt refused to accept his wife's sudden misgivings. Nothing he had seen, he insisted, had suggested that their lodger was anything more than what he had said he was, an unemployed Irishman looking for work. However, he did speak to Richards about the cupboard and, despite his protestations of innocence, forced him to fill in the hole he had so carefully made.

At the beginning of August, with his plans for household storage thwarted, Richards took over the rental of a nearby garden allotment using an alias. It was not an interest in horticulture that took him there – the allotment had a shed. This, Richards had decided, would be a safe enough place to store his growing stock of deadly chemicals. It was also far enough away from Clara Street's prying eyes to be used as a collection point for fellow IRA members when they needed to collect fresh supplies. It seemed to him to be a perfect solution and one that worked well for a week or so. But Richards was a careless terrorist. He did not seem to understand fully the volatile nature of the chemicals he was handling, and neither did any of his

Clara Street, Coventry. (Author's Collection)

clandestine callers. Potassium chlorate, a white powder, was eventually spilled across much of the shed's floor. Anyone visiting stood on it and carried it away on the soles of their shoes. But they, like Richards, seemed to share an ignorance of its destructive capability. On 13 August the inevitable happened. Two men arrived at the allotment and were allowed admittance to the storage shed. Carelessly Richards lit a cigarette and accidentally dropped his lighted match on to the floor. A frantic attempt to extinguish the flame failed, and just as the three men escaped through the door the shed blew up. More by luck than judgement, all three managed to escape unharmed.

While none of his fellow gardeners were able to put a name to a face, this explosion alerted Coventry police to a threat they had assumed would remain in the capital city. They quickly identified the residue of white powder on open ground that surrounded the burnt-out shed. Bomb experts confirmed that the chemical, apart from its deadly nature, was also a good indicator of IRA activity in the area. A six-month bombing campaign had left behind enough forensic evidence to create a terrorist profile. What they saw on the ground around the area of the allotment explosion was enough to convince them that a terrorist cell was somewhere nearby. Exactly where, however, was not going to be discovered for some time.

Lucky to escape with his life Richards wisely laid low for the following few days. Meanwhile, the IRA, alerted by the sudden and unexpected news coverage and concerned as to the fate of their Coventry link, decided to try and assess the damage done. On 21 August 32-year-old Peter Barnes, another IRA courier, was sent from London to discover whether or not James Richards had been arrested. He was also instructed to try and determine if the house at Clara Street was under surveillance. Born in Banagher, County Offaly, Barnes was immediately accepted by the Hewitts

Coventry railway station, regularly used by James Richards for his frequent trips to London.
(Author's Collection)

when he arrived in the late morning with the cover story that he too was unemployed but a good friend of their lodger. A brief look around the area satisfied him that the house was still safe, as was Richards. This, he then explained to his fellow conspirator, meant they would plant their next bomb in Coventry.

Richards told him he had no bomb-making materials. The shed explosion had destroyed everything. But Barnes was an explosives handler; his job had always been to convey explosives from central sources to those who made bombs. He assured Richards that he would provide all that was needed from London within two or three days. All he needed Richards to do was to provide him with a suitcase. This was difficult to do, as like everything else the suitcases he had once held at the house had also been blown up. So it was decided between the two of them to send Brigid out to buy a new one, telling her that it was needed because Richards had some clothes that he needed to send south. She accepted the reason, and also that when she made the purchase she must get a receipt, which she did. At about the same time, Mary, who was not working that day, was sent off to Celia's Cake Shop where she normally worked, to buy two hessian flour sacks. Barnes had explained to Richards that in order to carry the potassium chlorate inside the suitcase he needed something to package it in. He had used hessian sacks before and was happy to do so again. Unfortunately when Mary returned, the bags she had bought were too coarsely meshed and Barnes said they were unusable. He gave her back the 2s she had paid but took her receipt and added it to the one Brigid had collected with the suitcase earlier, and after ordering Richards to find some means of transport to carry the bomb he left for London.

With that thought in mind the next day Richards travelled by bus into Coventry. He needed something that was both familiar and yet inconspicuous. Something that would arouse no suspicion and was light and easy to move around, and more importantly had not been stolen. He chose a bicycle. After some deliberation at Halfords cycle shop, he paid a £5 deposit on a bicycle with a carrier basket attachment and agreed to collect it two days later.

On 24 August during the early afternoon an unknown Irishman arrived at Clara Street. This was the bomb maker; his identity has never been established and no alias was ever given to announce his arrival, but Brigid O'Hara was careful to ensure that with her son Joseph at work she, her daughter-in-law and the baby would go out while he was at the house. So, the family walked the streets until after 11 p.m.

The next day Richards was back at Halfords at just after midday. After paying the outstanding amount of 19s 6d he took the new bicycle and rode it back to Rugby. There he carefully parked it in the narrow back lane behind his lodgings and returned to his rooms. The mysterious Irishman arrived shortly afterwards and after making the finishing touches to his bomb he carried it out to the bicycle, carefully placed it into the basket and cycled off to Coventry.

Both Richards and Barnes believed the bomb would be placed well away from the public. The IRA had been reasonably careful over the preceding months to attack property and utility installations. It was probably reasonable for them to assume the same pattern would be followed, but the stranger pedalling his way into Coventry

Broadgate, Coventry, c. 1920. It would have looked much the same in 1939. (Author's Collection)

had no local knowledge. When he arrived in Broadgate, whether through panic or by design, he simply left the bicycle resting on the curb in front of a parked car outside Astley's shop and walked away.

Friday 25 August was market day, possibly the busiest day of the week. People had been arriving in the city throughout the morning. By the time the bicycle was being so carefully parked, hundreds were on the streets enjoying the warm summer weather. So when the 5lb bomb exploded at exactly 2.32 p.m., its impact was devastating: 81-year-old James Clay, schoolboy John Arnott, 50-year-old Gwilym Rolands, 33-year-old Rex Gentle and 21-year-old Elsie Ansell, who was two weeks away from her wedding, were all killed, and fifty others were injured.

The murder investigation that followed was meticulous. Police quickly found the remains of the bicycle used to ferry the bomb into the city crushed beneath the car that had been parked in front of it. Careful examination of the badly damaged frame and wheels revealed that the cycle's registration number had not been filed off. This piece of carelessness by the terrorists then led the investigation team to Halfords. From staff there they were able to establish a reasonably good description of the man who bought it and, perhaps more importantly, the key fact that this unknown man had travelled from Rugby.

Meanwhile, in London, a few days before the Coventry bomb, police had uncovered a plot to explode three other 5lb bombs in the capital by a terrorist group operating out of a flat in Leinster Gardens, Paddington. The targets were New Scotland Yard, Westminster Abbey and the Bank of England. About two hours before the Coventry explosion had taken place a raid on this flat had resulted in the arrest of four men. Caught after a rooftop chase, it was later discovered that the men had intended to use two tricycles and one bicycle to plant the bombs, which immediately suggested a probable connection with the Coventry explosion. Within two days London police had also uncovered the identity of the explosives supplier.

Peter Barnes had rented a flat close to Paddington and when police raided it on 27 August they found potassium chlorate hidden inside three packets labelled 'Shampoo Powder'. More damning was a letter. Sealed inside an envelope and with a Dublin address, it was intended for a man named Jim Kelly. When police read its contents they found it contained details of Barnes's movements across both England and Scotland and also gave specific information relating to the Coventry bomb. More importantly it was dated 24 August 1939, the day before the explosion in Broadgate. Barnes had obviously been too preoccupied to post it.

Faced with what appeared to be overwhelming evidence Barnes insisted he was not an IRA member nor had he any sympathies with their cause. The potassium chlorate he claimed had been bought innocently from a woman in London's Oxford Street. In his later statement he asserted that it was only when he had opened the packets that he had realised he had not bought shampoo. He was not believed.

With the letter in their possession the London police team knew they had at least one member of the Coventry terrorist group, but desperately needed further evidence to locate the base from which they had operated. The breakthrough finally came when Barnes admitted to having a second flat, which he claimed to have rented for his fiancée, Sarah Keane. The woman in question was quickly found and after an intensive search of the living accommodation so were two key receipts, one for a suitcase and one for two hessian flour sacks, both sold by Coventry shops before the bombing. The IRA it seemed maintained a strict accounting practice, damning for Barnes and all the evidence Coventry police needed.

The receipt for the sacks led them straight to Celia's Cake Shop and Mary Hewitt. On 28 August they went knocking on the door at 25 Clara Street. James Richards was still renting his rooms and a search of the house found more explosive materials. He was immediately arrested and on 2 September so too was Joseph Hewitt, his wife Mary and his mother Brigid O'Hara. Three weeks later, with police convinced that they had the Coventry terrorist cell, all were charged with murder along with Peter Barnes.

The trial opened on 11 December 1939 before Mr Justice Singleton and lasted for three days. Barnes continued to plead his innocence. Richards had no such intentions. He admitted from the outset that he was a member of the IRA and that he had taken part in the building of the bomb that had badly damaged or destroyed as many as forty-three Coventry businesses. The jury took thirty minutes to find both men guilty. In the case of the Hewitt family the jury returned a 'not guilty' verdict and accepted that their lodger had duped them. Richards gave a short speech to the court in which he thanked his defence team, claimed the explosions were part of a just cause and left the dock shouting, 'God bless Ireland.'

The pair were executed together at Birmingham on Wednesday 7 February 1940 by Thomas Pierrepoint.

14
THE WITCHCRAFT MURDER

Charles Walton, 74, had lived all his life in Lower Quinton, a village which in 1945 along with its near neighbours Upper Quinton and Admington, had a population of no more than 493, most of whom knew everything there was to know about their neighbours. A somewhat reclusive figure, Charles had lived alone for a number of years but in later life had begun to suffer badly from rheumatism. This no doubt had added to his sense of isolation and walking had become ever more difficult as the years went by. A quiet, inoffensive old man who had no known enemies in the village, he had continued to work whenever he could. Whitecross Farm had used him as a cowman and at the start of spring 1944 he had taken on the odd-job role for local farmer Alfred Potter. A widower since his wife's death in 1927, Walton had subsidised his income from the proceeds of a £297 inheritance she had

Charles Walton lived in one of these thatched cottages. (Author's Collection)

Meon Hill viewed from Upper Quinton. (Author's Collection)

left him in her will, but had been forced to relinquish some of his independence after it became obvious to his family that he needed help around the house. His niece Edith Walton, Edie to her friends, moved in shortly after the start of the war to help him cope. As she was employed nearby it was a perfect solution for both of them.

On Valentine's Day 1945, Charles Walton left home at 9 a.m. It was a fine, sunny day; his plan was to take advantage of the weather and cut hedges at a place known locally as the Hill grounds, a lonely spot on Meon Hill about a mile away. He carried with him a walking stick, his double-pronged hay fork and a sickle-shaped slash hook, and before leaving he had told Edie to expect him home by about 4 p.m. She never saw him alive again.

When she got back from work at 6 p.m. and realised her uncle had not been home she grew alarmed. Her first thoughts were that he had been taken ill or his rickety old legs had given out on him and that he might be lying out in the cold unable to make anyone hear. She roused next-door neighbour Harry Beasley and asked him to join her in a search. In fading light they did a quick walk around all the fields where they thought the old man would have worked that day, and after drawing a blank fetched Alfred Potter.

Potter expressed some surprise at their arrival and told Edie that he thought he had seen her uncle working on Meon Hill just after midday. When he had gone up to feed his cattle he was sure he had seen Walton in his shirtsleeves cutting the hedges some 500yds away. He then grabbed a torch and accompanied the pair out into the fields. By now it was completely dark outside; the three of them climbed slowly up the hill with Potter leading the way until he reached the hedgerow where he claimed to have seen Walton earlier in the day. The torchlight quickly picked out the old man's body laid in a shallow ditch close against the hedge. But Walton had not died of natural causes. Caught in the narrow beam of light it was obvious to all that he had been horrifically mutilated. Suddenly aware of Edie's presence Potter switched

The narrow lane that leads from Upper Quinton on to Meon Hill. (Author's Collection)

the torch off and told Beasley to take her back down the hill and call the police while he stayed with the body. Edith took little persuading.

Police constable Lomansney was first on the scene. According to his later statement Walton was fully dressed but his clothing was unbuttoned at the front and his trouser braces were undone at the front and broken at the back. His cap was lying under his head; there was a watch chain in his waistcoat pocket but no watch, neither was there any money on his person. He had been savagely attacked with the slash hook, which had struck him three times in all and was still embedded in his body. This had resulted in the severing of all the main arteries in his neck, which had probably killed him, and then his own hay fork had been driven through the neck, pinning the body to the ground. A more detailed examination in daylight also revealed that a cross had been roughly hewn into the chest and neck.

Warwickshire's Detective Superintendent Alex Spooner took control of the case and after organising a detailed forensic search had the body moved. Later post-mortem results added little to what was already known other than Walton had suffered numerous cuts to his hands and arms as he attempted to fend off his attacker. More interestingly, a fingerprint check of the weapons used in the killing revealed Alfred Potter's prints on the slash hook handle. When questioned Potter explained them away after he told the superintendent that he had tried to remove the hook from Walton's chest while he was alone with the body. At that point, two days into the investigation, Spooner handed the case over to Scotland Yard.

They sent the man who eventually became the country's most famous detective, Robert Fabian. A later 1950s television series based loosely around his career, *Fabian of the Yard*, would assure his invincible reputation as a detective and ensure his name ranked alongside such fictional greats as Sherlock Holmes. Ultimately the name itself would become synonymous with Scotland Yard. But when he arrived in Lower Quinton that reputation was still being earned. Nevertheless, his arrival was

The road linking Upper and Lower Quinton. Charles Walton's route on the day of his death. (Author's Collection)

still much heralded by the press, and he brought with him an enviable record of success. Accompanied by the very able Detective Inspector Webb he was also astute enough to recognise the abilities of Alex Spooner and between the three of them they formed the nucleus of an extremely discerning and effective murder team.

With post-mortem details that clearly showed the attack may have been frenzied but not without warning, Fabian was quick to form the hypothesis that Walton had been killed by someone he knew. The evidence in support of that was, he argued, easy to assess. Defence wounds were a clear indicator that he had seen and faced his attacker. The location of the attack – where he had been working – suggested the killer was local. The hedgerow was at an isolated place not used by the general public and on private land without easy access. At the time of the murder Walton must have stopped cutting the hedge and placed the slash hook on the ground. No evidence of a struggle or a fight had been found, so it was reasonable to assume that he had met and quite possibly spoken to his killer. All his clothing had been pulled open but he had not been stripped. There were two possible explanations for this. One, that he had subsequently been robbed or, two, that the killer wanted to create the notion that robbery had been a motive. Finally, the missing watch; if it had been stolen simply because it had broken at the time of the attack then the killer was a local man. Why else be concerned over time? But if creating an alibi was crucial then the time fixed by the watch was equally crucial. If it had not been a local man why steal the watch at all? It had no value; it was neither silver nor gold – and why leave behind the chain? The first local on Fabian's list was Alfred Potter.

Potter became a serious suspect for a number of reasons. The first was that he had said quite openly that on the day of the murder he had seen Charles Walton in his shirtsleeves, at around midday, cutting a hedgerow some 500yds away. Fabian knew, because he had received the pathologist's report, that when the dead man's clothing was removed his shirt was found to be sleeveless. Potter had also handled the murder weapon after discovering the body when he should have known that to do so would contaminate the murder scene. He had also given police conflicting accounts of his movements on the day of the killing and by his own admission had told the investigation team that no one other than Walton and himself usually went into the field where the body was found. Unfortunately for the farmer he had no exonerating alibi to quash the suspicion, though perversely neither was there any contrary corroborating evidence to support Fabian's hunch.

The investigation area slowly widened and after fruitless door-to-door enquiries in the village and in the surrounding area police moved to the nearby prisoner-of-war camp at Long Marston. Here, in line with other British camps, there was no rigorous security. It contained 1,043 prisoners – mainly Slavs, Italians, Germans and a few from the Ukraine – and all had limited freedom to move around the local countryside. For a while an Italian serviceman was held on suspicion after it was discovered that he had bloodstains on his overcoat. Forensic tests, however, eventually revealed that the blood had belonged to a rabbit and the man was released.

On 20 March 1945 the inquest into Charles Walton's death was opened at Stratford-upon-Avon. For the first time much of the known evidence was aired in public and those prominent in police enquiries were brought to court to give their evidence, a key figure being Alfred Potter. He was questioned at length by South West Warwickshire coroner, Mr G.F. Lodder and gave the court a brief account of his association with the murdered man.

> He [Walton] had been employed by the firm of which I [Potter] was a partner. He had been employed for about nine months and was paid 1s 6d an hour. He had no regular hours but worked when he liked and knocked off when he liked. . . . I don't know whether Walton carried any money with him, but I never saw him with more than £1 in any case. . . . I did not see Walton in the early morning but saw someone I thought was Walton at about 12.30. I could not swear it was him . . . I went to the College Arms with a Mr Stanley at about a quarter to twelve and remained there until about twelve o'clock and then returned to Mr Stanley's farm, where for about ten minutes, we stood looking at a tractor that was being repaired. I then went back home, put down some tools I had been using, and walked up the hill to see the sheep and calves and fed the cattle. That was when I saw Walton about 500 yards away, or someone I took to be Walton. It was someone with his jacket off. I particularly noticed the man was in his shirtsleeves.

At that point the coroner interrupted and asked if he were aware that Charles Walton had worn a sleeveless shirt. Potter acknowledged that he did, but insisted that he must have seen him with his sleeves rolled up.

> Anyone working would have his sleeves rolled up . . . I never saw the whole of him, only the shirt sleeves, thought it was him, and turned and went home . . . I remained home for about five minutes and then helped Batchelor, another man, to pulp mangolds. When we had finished it was one o'clock and I went in to dinner.

Potter went on to detail his movements throughout the afternoon including dragging a heifer out of a ditch.

At that point Fabian stood and asked the coroner pointedly to question Potter more closely about the timing of his arrival at that ditch and told the court that the farmer was telling the court a different story to the one he had told police officers. What the detective inspector was alluding to was a statement made by Potter in which he had said that he had fed the cows and dragged the heifer from the ditch much earlier. Potter then confirmed that his earlier statement had been incorrect and that he had simply been confused.

Later in the hearing Edie Walton was able to confirm that her uncle had not carried any money with him when he left the house and that that was his normal routine. But the watch, she insisted, he had always carried about his person. Other than these facts nothing else came out of the coroner's court hearing and the inevitable verdict of murder was returned.

From this point onwards the investigation into the murder of Charles Walton began to flounder and eventually it ground to a halt. Police had no firm evidence on which either to act or to build a case against anyone. Nothing of any use to the murder team came from those who lived in the village, and nothing new was to be gleaned from the body itself. Rumours concerning the motive behind the murder inevitably began to circulate among those who knew the area and rapidly spread to outlying villages. Before the year was at an end it had become a recorded and therefore acceptable fact that Walton's murder had been a witchcraft killing. There was no evidence to support the theory, and the supposition that the killing had all the hallmarks of some sort of satanic ritual was completely without foundation. But someone – possibly the murderer – does appear to have revisited the scene on more than one occasion throughout 1945 in order that the witchcraft rumours be reinforced.

Fabian was reported as having encountered a black dog one evening at dusk as he walked the ground around Meon Hill. It apparently ran past him and disappeared into the gathering twilight. Unknown to him at the time was the legend of the spectral dog of Lower Quinton. The minute this seemingly innocuous encounter became public knowledge it was interpreted as an evil portent, and when a police car killed a dog later that week fiction became fact. At the murder site within days of this portentous meeting a dead dog was found hanging from a tree. This led on to a dead cow in a ditch and letters from people far and wide claiming knowledge of witchcraft activities and coven meetings in and around the village. Substance was then given to the rumour and speculation after it became known that the sign of the cross had been cut into Charles Walton's chest. From that point on there was little cooperation from the villagers and Fabian became well aware that this was to be one murder he would never solve.

Even today, Meon Hill is considered by some to be a mystical area. Nearby sit the Rollright Stones shrouded in mystery and magic, visited over the years by the curious, the strange and no doubt the evil. Legend has it that a king from Europe and his soldiers were marching through the countryside intent on conquering England when they happened across a strange old woman. She offered the king a challenge: 'Seven long

The Rollright Stones. (Author's Collection)

strides shalt thou take, if Long Compton thou canst see King of England thou shalt be.' He accepted the challenge and made the seven strides, but found his view blocked by a hill, as the old hag knew it would be: 'As Long Compton thou canst not see, King of England thou shalt not be. Rise up stick, and stand still stone, for King of England thou shalt be none. Thou and thy men hoar stones shall be and myself an eldern tree.'

So was formed, folklore would have it, the stone circle seen today and as with anything of this type and age it became a magnet for druids, astronomers and witches alike. Add to this the history of witchcraft believed to have been practised in this part of Warwickshire for centuries and one begins to understand the Scotland Yard detective's frustration, though Fabian almost certainly never believed that witchcraft had anything to do with the horrific murder of Charles Walton.

Not so a number of modern writers, who have claimed that the killing mirrored that of Ann Turner who was brutally murdered by local farmer James Heywood. So brutal was the killing that according to a number of texts, many reportedly given to Fabian, he pinned her to the ground with a hayfork and carved a cross on her body. Such nonsense has added to the witchcraft element of the case over the years. In author Stephen Knight's account of the killing in *Perfect Murder*, published by Grafton Books in 1987, he claimed the motive was far more mundane and that Fabian knew exactly who had committed the murder from the outset of his investigations. What prevented the killer from being brought to court was simple lack of evidence. The motive of course was money.

Since the murder a theory with some credibility has evolved, which Stephen Knight explored. The speculation was that Walton had money at home, a significant amount for the time, and that he loaned some or possibly all to a local farmer and agreed a date by when the debt would be repaid. The time for payment came and went, and after an argument between the two men in the field on Meon Hill on the morning of 14 February, in a fit of anger the farmer killed the moneylender. The murderer then made a hurried search of Walton's body to retrieve his IOUs, before inflicting a wound

*Lower Quinton church where
Charles Walton was buried.*
(Author's Collection)

he knew would arouse fear and suspicion locally: the sign of the cross. Among people who believed in superstition and witchcraft, committing such an act was certain to cause confusion and fear. No doubt it worked very well. All that remained was to create signs of satanic rites where none existed and the black magic motive was reinforced.

The theory has some merit, yet there is little evidence to support the notion that Walton had any significant wealth. Certainly he may have saved over the years, but although he had a bank account, there was almost nothing in it, and all the signs were that he was far from wealthy. That does not mean he did not have the means to loan small amounts of money and small amounts may have been all it took. Murder to hide a debt that one cannot repay is perhaps a reasonable motive in the absence of anything better.

Whether Fabian would have believed this hypothesis is not known. Though he published his memoirs he never allowed himself the luxury of expressing an opinion or giving credence to his own thoughts on the case. All that is known is that he returned to London some two months after his much vaunted arrival in Warwickshire a disappointed man. He had been sure that he would discover the killer's identity when he set out, but the reticence of the villagers and persistent speculation from the press about the involvement of witchcraft had dogged his investigation throughout. Even an attempt to hold a séance at the scene of the murder in February 1952 failed when no medium could be found to take part.

Alex Spooner continued to visit the village and the murder site on the anniversary of the killing each year for the rest of his police career. He believed his presence would one day be rewarded by the truth, but he was wrong.

As a footnote to the murder, in 1960, after builders demolished outbuildings behind Charles Walton's cottage, a pocket watch was discovered in the rubble. It appeared to match the watch police had sought so desperately fifteen years earlier. If it had belonged to Charles Walton then either he had never worn it on the day of his murder or the killer had simply returned it to where it belonged.

15

THE RING OF BELLS MURDER

Coventry, 1945

When 68-year-old Amy Davis's husband Charlie died in 1941 she resolved to carry on doing what she had spent a large part of her life doing – running the Ring of Bells public house. With the war only two years old those closest to her saw it as a sensible decision, though they all had reservations about her safety in a city that had already seen its fair share of bombing. But for Amy there was nowhere other than Coventry she would rather be and it was a decision she never regretted. The regulars liked her, takings were generally good and she had a network of friends to call on whenever she needed help, and having her elder brother, Alderman Fred Lee, living around the corner was an added bonus. A civic dignitary in the family increased her standing in the local community and added a little kudos to her status as landlady, which she embraced wholeheartedly: being sister to a man of consequence gave her a number of advantages should they ever be needed, though it did not save her life.

Throughout the war years Amy had established a number of routines. These ensured the pub was always well stocked, well maintained, and well staffed on the days that mattered. They also ensured that cash was always banked on a daily basis and the day's takings removed from the cash till at the close of business. Only pennies were ever left in the bar; the rest was taken up to her bedroom for safe storage overnight. But Amy did not possess a safe. She believed living above the pub rendered that unnecessary and so cash always spent the night beside her bed. The routine was habitual and well known among those who used the bar. That knowledge cost Amy her life.

On the morning of 24 October 1945 cleaner Mary Geelan found the doors locked when she arrived to carry out the morning chores before lunchtime opening. After a frustrating few minutes she realised the door bolts were still in place and understandably presumed that Amy had probably taken ill during the night. In a panic she ran to fetch Amy's brother Fred Lee who lived nearby and he followed her back to the pub and managed to force an entry. After a few loud shouts and a quick search he found Amy's body in the empty bath. She was fully clothed and had been brutally beaten about the head in what can only be described as a frenzied attack; her face had then been covered over with a towel.

Coventry's Detective Superintendent Pendleton was on the scene within an hour. He quickly established that the motive for the killing had been robbery. The cash register in the bar had been forced, though with some difficulty. A poker, knife, scissors and a pair of pliers had all played a part and had been carelessly discarded in turn as each proved inadequate to the task. Empty cash bags littered the floor around the bar area and in Amy's bedroom the Gladstone bag, which normally held the previous night's takings, had been taken from its usual place beneath her bed and was open and empty. Further searches of the upstairs rooms discovered her handbag, which had also been stripped of any money, and most of her jewellery was missing. Brother Fred was able to tell police that among the jewellery stolen had been a gold wristwatch, which Amy's husband had given to her in 1924, and three gold rings.

A later forensic search of the building showed no evidence of a forced entry and it was concluded that the killer had probably left through a window. A careful examination of all doors and windows had revealed no tell-tale signs of force anywhere in the downstairs bar area. This led the police investigation team to form the hypothesis that Amy's attacker had possibly never left the bar after closing. When further enquiries among the pub's regulars revealed her as a creature of habit it appeared to lend credence to the fact that her killer had more than likely been a stranger; a regular would have known to leave the cash register alone.

On 3 November a bloodstained hammer was discovered on waste ground near to the pub and forensic tests confirmed the blood had come from the Ring of Bells' landlady. At the inquest five weeks later Professor J.M. Webster, director of the West Midlands Forensic Science Laboratory, was able to tell the coroner that this had definitely been the murder weapon. From the wounds on her head he was also able to reconstruct in some detail just how the attack had taken place. He told the court that his post-mortem examination had revealed that Amy had first been hit from behind. That single blow, in his opinion, had been struck while she stood in the bathroom and as her body fell it had slipped into the empty bath. There her killer had simply rained blows down upon her head in an attempt to kill her, but she had actually died as a result of secondary injuries caused by strangulation.

Gilbert Street today.
(Author's Collection)

There the case came to an almost abrupt end. Hundreds of statements, countless suspects and numerous newspaper articles failed to reveal the killer or elicit sufficient information to cause an arrest. The case dropped from public view and was eventually filed away as unsolved. Then, several years later, a letter arrived at Coventry police headquarters purporting to know the killer's identity:

> On October 24 me and my mate Charlie had been drinking in the Brewer and Baker and the Albert in Gilbert Street. We were both short of money and Charlie said, 'I know how we can get some money off Amy.' He used to know Charlie Davis and Amy well.
>
> I met him in the passage at the Ring of Bells. He opened his coat and showed me a funny looking hammer. . . . He told me to go while he hid upstairs and to come back after closing time. He gave me something to force the register and while I was doing it I heard a scream from upstairs. . . . Amy was half in and half out of the bath. . . . He tried to strangle her and then she stopped moaning. . . . He washed himself with a towel and put it over her face.

It had the ring of truth about it but offered up no new facts. Police were sceptical and eventually declared it a hoax. Their argument was that while it appeared to confirm the theory that had been postulated at the time it offered nothing new and, as they told the *Coventry Evening Telegraph*, much of what was written could have been gleaned from the various press reports. But this was not necessarily so. The idea that two men could have been involved in the murder may not have been new to police but it certainly was to the general public. In all the newspaper reports at the time no suggestion had ever been made that more than one killer could have been involved. Yet it did make a good deal of sense. Unmoved, police put the case back in the unsolved file and there it stayed until 1988. At that juncture a second letter, this time from a different hand, was sent to the Coventry police stating that the killer had worked as an odd-job man for Amy and his first name began with the letter F. No other details were given and this was the last piece of correspondence ever received. The case remains open.

The Brewer & Baker pub today.
(Author's Collection)

16
A WARTIME ARGUMENT

Coventry, 1950

When 34-year-old Elizabeth Byrne walked into the Acorn public house on 10 July 1950 she had intended to do no more than have a quiet drink. After being on her feet all day behind the counter of the local bakery shop, the drink and the seat by the bar were much needed. Attractive and blonde, she was a regular at most of the pubs around her home on Gosford Street, knew most of the locals and occasionally drank with some of them. The combination of hair and good looks had earned her the sobriquet of Blondie, to which she raised no objection. Never meant unkindly she accepted it for what it was, a compliment to her looks, leastways that was how she liked to view it and why not? It earned her the odd free drink, which she was usually happy to accept, a cigarette to go with it and from time to time good conversation, though she would probably have been among the first to admit that one did not necessarily follow the other.

Gosford Street has all but disappeared. (Author's Collection)

That night, however, her luck appeared to be in. Strangers in the shape of Francis Mudd and Norman Bradshaw, both from Liverpool, met her the moment she walked in through the door. The two men had arrived in Coventry some four weeks earlier seeking a change in fortune, believing Coventry offered them better work prospects than the north-west. Elizabeth found them easy company and the three of them stayed together until closing time, at which point Bradshaw, who had no lodging set up for the night, asked her if she had a spare bed.

Transient labour in 1950 was not uncommon. The country had been ravaged by war for six years and industry was still rebuilding. For large numbers of ex-servicemen that meant they took work wherever they could find it and when it came to an end they moved on. Most people, having endured the horrors of nightly bombing, had grown accustomed to helping those around them and so Elizabeth had no qualms about giving up a spare room, but told him it would just be the one night. A grateful Bradshaw, who had a job working close by as a switchboard operator, and needed a clear head on the following morning, agreed the terms and followed her home.

Bradshaw was as good as his word. Next day he was away long before she left for work at the baker's shop, and Elizabeth saw no more of either of the two men until Friday 14 July. At 10.30 p.m. that night she was at home with a man named Ralph Doherty when they turned up unexpectedly. Surprised at finding them on her doorstep she nevertheless invited them in. At first all seemed to be well. She made the introductions and the three men began to talk about their wartime experiences. All three had fought abroad in the war. Mudd and Bradshaw had served in the army in France and talked about it readily enough. But Doherty, apart from volunteering the information that he had been in the RAF in Africa, refused to discuss his service in similar detail. Mudd began to get angry. He demanded that Doherty tell him where in Africa he had been posted but Doherty refused and told them it was none of their business. What had begun as a friendly chat suddenly turned ugly. Mudd, a powerfully built man, became aggressive and began to shout. Dismissive of Doherty's role in the war he cast doubt on the man's service record, called him a liar and pointed an accusing finger. Startled by this sudden burst of moral outrage Elizabeth told Mudd he had said enough and ordered him to leave. The argument would probably have ended at that point had Doherty remained silent but he could not resist one last sarcastic jibe as the two men made for the door. Equating Mudd's sudden exit to that of the army's retreat from Dunkirk he waved a dismissive hand in their direction. It was too much for Joseph Mudd. Pushing Elizabeth out of the way, he suddenly lunged at Doherty, who had not moved from the settee, and struck him a heavy blow to the head with his fist. It knocked Doherty backwards but before he could react Mudd struck him again several times.

Elizabeth made a dash for the street but was stopped by Bradshaw who slammed the front door shut and threw the bolt. As the two of them wrestled he managed to pinion her arms behind her back and push her against a wall. But she refused to be an easy victim and began to scream for next-door neighbour Jim Bearder. Desperate to silence her Bradshaw tried to gag her with his right hand but found it impossible to keep hold of her arms at the same time and was forced to let her go. Free of his grip she screamed ever louder and began to pummel her fists against the wall separating the house from her neighbours. Panicked by her defiance and voluble protest Bradshaw decided to run. With an urgent shout to Mudd to follow him he dragged Elizabeth away from the door, pulled the bolt back and ran out into the street. Mudd quickly followed suit and Doherty, who by this time had suffered horrific injuries to his face and head, was left to die.

Distressed, traumatised and in a state of near collapse Elizabeth then seemed to be seized by panic. When she realised Doherty had been so badly injured that he was unlikely to survive she became irrational. When her neighbours got to the door she slammed it shut and refused them entry. With her back pressed against it she shouted out that she was all right, that it had all been a mistake then waited for them to leave. What had suddenly scared her was the thought that they would find Doherty's body – in her house, and on her settee. Inexplicably she felt responsible, though at that stage Doherty was still breathing.

When Elizabeth eventually realised this she made an attempt to revive him with water but it was too little too late. There was nothing that anyone could have done for the man without expert medical attention, which was the one thing Elizabeth seemed too scared to go and fetch. Instead, after some deliberation she decided to go out and find the police; 200yds from the house she changed her mind and turned back, no doubt because she had realised she would be implicated in a murder. At that juncture she met Francis Mudd a second time. He was coming from the direction of her home and when they met she told him Doherty was dying. Mudd appeared unimpressed and told her it was her problem, not his, then went on his way as if he had done nothing wrong.

Back at the house Elizabeth found the front door wide open and Doherty no longer on the settee but unconscious on the floor. For ten minutes or so she sat with him and waited for him to die. When she was satisfied that he had given his last breath, under cover of darkness she dragged his body out of the house, across the street and into the ruins of a bombed-out building opposite. There she left him and walked the streets until dawn when she returned home, changed her clothes and went to work.

But Elizabeth had been careless. After she had placed the body among the bomb debris she had made no attempt to hide it. Neither had she wiped up the blood trail that had followed her across the street. In her desperation to be rid of the dead man none of these things had registered their importance. Distress and fear had made her incautious. At half-past seven that same morning neighbour Jim Bearder went out to feed his pet rabbits. It was he who found the body of Ralph Doherty after following a trail of blood that led all the way to the bombed-out buildings opposite his house. According to Professor Webster, the west Midlands forensic expert, Doherty had been dead no more than six or seven hours.

Police began the routine of door-to-door enquiries and by the end of the day Elizabeth was in custody. Too much noise had been made during the attack on Doherty and too many neighbours were able to point a finger in her

TWO MEN ON COVENTRY MURDER CHARGE

Woman Shop Assistant Accused – 'Concealment'

TWO young men and a 34 years old woman shop assistant appeared before Coventry City Magistrates to-day to face charges arising from the death of Ralph Doherty (39), whose body was found in debris in a doorway of a Gosford Street court on Saturday morning.

Accused of the murder of Doherty — a fitter and an ex-R.A.F. cook, who lived at 36, Dulverton Avenue, Coventry — were Francis Joseph Mudd (24), pipelayer, and Norman Vincent Bradshaw (22), switchboard operator. Their address was given by the police as 74, King George's Avenue, Coventry.

With them in the dock was Elizabeth Byrne, of 11 court, No. 2 house, Gosford Street. She was charged with "being present when certain persons unknown feloniously did murder Ralph Doherty on July 14 at Coventry and knowing the said persons and intending to obstruct and hinder the due course of law and justice, unlawfully and wilfully did conceal the said felony."

Brief Appearance

The three were in court for two minutes and were formally remanded in custody until next Tuesday by the Bench, comprising Alderman A. R. Grindlay (chairman), Mr. J. E. Parbury and Mr. Cyril Taylor.

Detective Superintendent W. Groom, applying for the remand, said: "The case will take some days to prepare and papers will have to be submitted to the Director of Public Prosecutions."

After the men had asked for legal aid, Superintendent Groom said: "They have been in Coventry only a few weeks and would not know any local members of the legal profession."

Mr. W. Wilson, who was in court, then offered to undertake the cases.

Asked by the Clerk, Mr. A. N. Murdoch, whether he could also undertake the defence of Byrne, Mr. Wilson said he was willing to do so unless it proved necessary for her to be separately represented.

Half an hour before the three accused were called, a queue of more than 100, including many women shoppers, were lined along the pavement outside St. Mary's Hall awaiting admission to the small crypt courtroom. Police officers were stationed in the courtyard to marshal those seeking admission.

Stockinged Feet

Those who could not gain admission to the court waited in the rain for a glimpse of the prisoners as they were escorted from the cells along a corridor and across the courtyard into the crypt.

Mudd and Bradshaw were in stockinged feet.

The Chief Constable, Mr. E. W. C. Pendleton, to-day thanked the Press for their co-operation. "I wish to express my appreciation of the speedy and accurate Press reporting of this case, which went a long way in bringing about these arrests after the description of the wanted people had been circulated," he said.

Headlines on Monday 17 July 1950. (Coventry Evening Telegraph) direction. She made no attempt to hide her involvement, quite probably she was relieved at her arrest, and within hours of police arriving at her door Francis Mudd and Norman Bradshaw joined her at Coventry police station. Twenty four-hours later all three stood in the dock before Coventry city magistrates. The two men were charged with murder and Elizabeth with being present and concealing the body. All pleaded not guilty and were remanded until August.

At the inquest, which opened on Wednesday 19 July, Professor Webster told the coroner that Doherty had died as a result of shock and concussion caused by severe violence. In effect the man had been beaten to death but, he added, there had been secondary injuries. Most of the blows he had received had been to the head but there was clear bruising to the muscle of the neck. In the professor's opinion Doherty had at some stage been kicked, which had badly bruised the front of his spine. This single piece of evidence was to have severe repercussions for Mudd. Elizabeth Byrne had never veered from her version of events and in her statement to police, made shortly after her arrest, had insisted Doherty never managed to get off the settee during the attack. The clear implication, of course, was that someone must have kicked him at some time after the initial assault. Of the three involved only Mudd had been thought to have returned to the house. Elizabeth had met him after her abortive search for the police and had found the front door open when she had arrived back home. Despite his denial that he had caused the injury found at the post-mortem examination, speculation over his guilt was no doubt heightened.

For Joseph Mudd the spectre of the gallows loomed large, but not so for his fellow prisoners. Elizabeth Byrne was released without charge on 2 August and collapsed in the dock when told that the Director of Public Prosecutions had decided to proceed no further. Prosecuting counsel, Mr Lewis, told magistrates that as a result of a recent case heard by the Court of Criminal Appeal, unless a charge of being an accessory after the fact could be sustained, misprision was no longer law and so the offence was to be considered virtually defunct. Two weeks later Bradshaw was brought back

The old County Hall, Coventry, once the home of the prison governor. (Author's Collection)

before magistrates and set free after the prosecution declared that no prima facie case had been proved, though chairman Alderman Vincent Wyles, apparently disappointed at the decision, was not prepared to release him without allowing himself the opportunity to express his displeasure over the prosecution's failure: 'You acted in a most cowardly manner and saw a fellow man punched to death. I would like to see you punished for this. I hope you will think of this for the rest of your days.'

Mudd's trial, held in Birmingham, began at 10 a.m. on 14 December 1950. The first day was spent hearing evidence from expert witnesses and those directly involved with the killing. All of it had been heard before at the magistrates' hearing and nothing new was brought into court. Mudd himself was called to give evidence in his own defence after lunch on the second day. He contended that he remembered almost nothing of the attack. According to his testimony he had been drinking on the night of Doherty's murder and that had caused some sort of amnesia. He told the jury that he had no memory of going to Elizabeth Byrne's house. He recalled having seen Doherty at some point and had a vague recollection of a settee but remembered little else. Under skilful questioning from his defence counsel he explained that he and Bradshaw had been drinking from 6 p.m. until they had arrived at the house in Gosford Street at some time after 10.30. There followed an argument of sorts between himself and the murdered man and he accepted that he had thrown a punch. He claimed then to know nothing else until he found himself sitting on a wall in Foleshill bus depot later that same night. There was nothing else he could add and despite enduring a vigorous cross-examination from the prosecution team he said little else.

In his summing up at the end of the trial Mr Justice Sellers told the jurors that they were to decide whether they accepted that Mudd had inflicted all the injuries found on Doherty's body. If they believed that to be true then they were bound by law to return a guilty verdict. The evidence of Elizabeth Byrne, he told them, had to be considered with some care. In his opinion her reliability as a witness should be questioned and she could be considered as having acted in an unreliable manner. The key decision, he went on, was simply one of guilt. Did they believe Mudd had caused the death by his violent actions? If they did, then had the amount of alcohol he had consumed caused him to act out of character and without intent to kill? If this was to be their accepted view then they were to return a verdict of manslaughter.

It took the jury three-quarters of an hour to agree that he had been guilty of murder. He was duly sentenced to death. But Mudd was fortunate in his defence team. Local Coventry solicitor Mr Wilson, who had operated in an advisory capacity at the trial, launched an appeal a week after the verdict had been announced. He argued in a letter to the Home Secretary that while Mudd had struck the killer blows, it had not been premeditated and he had used no weapon. He contended that death had resulted because Francis Mudd was a man of great strength and there had been provocation. But he conceded that the conviction for murder was just. What he required of the Home Office was mercy. It was forthcoming and on the morning of 30 December, three days before he was due to be executed, a reprieve was granted and the sentence commuted to one of life imprisonment.

17

THE SILENCING OF PENELOPE MOGANO

Coventry, 1954

Penelope Phyllis Mogano was known to her neighbours as the woman who danced, on account of her lifelong interest in old-time dancing. Born in Ryde on the Isle of Wight, she had spent twenty-three of her forty-four years in Coventry where her husband was employed as a works inspector for Daimler. She and Carlo had married in 1931. It was a good marriage and in 1938 their first son, Michael, was born, and two years later a brother, Adrian, followed. In 1951 the family moved to Holland Road where they quickly established themselves among the local community and formed strong friendships with fellow dancers at the nearby Savoy old-time dancing club. They were well respected by neighbours and considered by most to be comfortably off; a view Penelope had helped foster through her sense of style and fashion. Never seen outside the house unless impeccably dressed, over the years she had built up a comprehensive wardrobe of clothes and wore them well. She was house-proud and her home reflected her tastes. Much of every day was spent in maintaining the high standards she had set herself. Carlo certainly provided well for his family.

Like most other families at that time the household had a routine. During the working week Penelope would do most of her household chores during the morning. She would then prepare lunch for her sons who would arrive back from school at about 1 p.m. Carlo would join them at about the same time and the family would always sit down and eat together. The afternoons were generally free and Penelope would begin preparing the evening meal at about 5.30. It was a routine that had been established almost from the outset of her marriage, and it was one she had grown accustomed to and possibly enjoyed.

Apart from her eldest son having left school to work as a hairdresser at Coventry police headquarters, Monday 18 January 1954 began in exactly the same way as all the previous Mondays. But life for the Mogano family was never to be the same again.

When 14-year-old Adrian arrived home from his school's afternoon session at about 4.50 he found the house in darkness and all the doors locked. It was unexpected and Adrian knew that it could not have been planned. If his mother had intended to be home late she would have told him at lunchtime. So, as he kicked his

Bablake school where the Mogano children were educated. (Author's Collection)

heels in the cold and the minutes passed by, his sense of concern deepened. When his father arrived at the house an hour later, concern turned to apprehension. Carlo probably shared his son's disquiet. He knew his wife well enough to know she was a creature of habit. To leave her son outside on a freezing night was totally out of character, so when he turned his key in the lock of the back door it was with a very real sense of fear.

He found the kitchen neat and tidy with all the crockery used at lunchtime washed and neatly put away. Oddly, there were no signs of food having been prepared for the evening meal, which he would have expected. In the lounge everything was as it had been when he returned to work after lunch; nothing had been moved or disturbed. All the household chores had been completed, the brasses polished, the furniture dusted and the fire grate cleaned and set for the evening. At that point it no doubt seemed his earlier concerns were unfounded and that his wife had simply been delayed somewhere. So probably no need to worry, Monday's meal would just be late. But when he flicked on the light switch of the dining room he knew that none of that was true. What met his sight as the light flooded the room would haunt him all his days. His wife was sitting in an easy chair, obviously dead. Her blood was splattered over the walls, ceiling and floor. On her lap was a 12in carving knife, which had clearly caused a number of her injuries. Twenty-five blows to her head meant her skull had been smashed to pieces and her face had been horrifically mutilated.

The view towards what was the Mogano house. The house lies behind the trees and the killer could well have approached unnoticed. (Author's Collection)

Scotland Yard Detective Superintendent John Edmunds and Detective Sergeant Ted Williams travelled from London within hours of the local police's arrival at the house. With the help of a forensic team they quickly established that Penelope Mogano had been attacked with two weapons: the knife, found on her body, and some kind of round-headed hammer, which had caused the serious head wounds. Quite probably she had also been intending to go out that afternoon. In the main bedroom a clean, unworn dress had been found laid across the bed. The post-mortem examination revealed there had been no sexual assault. Forensic examination appeared to show nothing in the house had been touched or disturbed, and the killer appeared to have locked the door behind him as he left. Motive was going to be much harder to establish.

Initial suspicion naturally centred on husband Carlo Mogano, but it was quickly established that he had no involvement in his wife's death. Nevertheless he was crucial to police enquiries; only he could furnish them with the background detail they needed to better understand his wife's past, usual routines and friendships. Throughout the night following his discovery of the murder he stayed at Coventry police headquarters and offered what assistance he could. From these discussions and information gleaned from ongoing door-to-door enquiries among the Moganos' neighbours, detectives were able to build up a reasonably accurate picture of Penelope Mogano and the life she had led.

When Carlo had discovered her body she was wearing what were described as 'house clothes covered by an apron'. Among all the information offered up by her husband and corroborated by her neighbours was one crucial fact. Penelope's high personal standards meant she would never have left the house dressed in that manner. Likewise neither would she have opened the front door to a caller. This meant that in all probability whoever killed her went into the house through the back door and quite likely knew her. By the following day, with reasonable accuracy, police were also able to confirm the time of the killing. The dress laid out on the bed proved to be more significant than they had first imagined. Carlo told the inquiry team that he and Penelope were extremely friendly with a Sidney Worrall and his wife. On the afternoon of her murder she was to have walked to the Worralls' house to take tea at 3 p.m. She would have changed into the dress before she left. Police knew from both Carlo and his son Adrian that Penelope had been alive and well at 2 p.m. when they both left after eating lunch, and that she had obviously planned to keep her date at the Worralls'; therefore, the murder had to have taken place between two and three that same afternoon. This supposition was later supported in part by fact. When the post-mortem results were completed, while they did not fully concur with this hypothesis, they did estimate time of death as being no later than 4 p.m. Allowing for some latitude in this time assessment, the Scotland Yard men felt enough circumstantial evidence existed to support their earlier opinion.

On Wednesday 20 January 1954, two days after the murder, police attempted to re-create the scene inside the Mogano home before the killer struck and then re-enact the murder. Using the limited forensic evidence available, and with the help of a forensic expert brought in from London, they endeavoured to plot the killer's movements from the moment the back door had been opened. In fact, the method of entry was the first key debating point. There was an argument prevalent at the time that Mrs Mogano had never opened the door to her killer but that he or she had gained entry without her knowledge. This theory was not without its supporters but was not necessarily supported by the post-mortem evidence. Defensive wounds to the arms and hands suggested that the killer and the victim had been face to face, not something that would have happened had the killer made an unseen entry. Surely, ran the argument, had that been the case then she would have been struck down from behind and probably died having never seen her killer's face. The police team examined the notion closely and though they never discarded it as a possibility they also never gave it a deal of credence.

Bassett Road, once home of the Worralls. The house lies on the right just beyond the bend. (Author's Collection)

It seems that from the outset the investigating team were probably convinced that, on the weight of evidence, she had let the killer into the house. Recreating the murder scene allowed them to explore the possibility that Penelope Mogano had first been struck while standing. As she fell back into the easy chair in which she eventually died she had then been hit viciously about the head with a hammer. Only after her death had the facial mutilations been carried out. This then threw up three possible theories. One, that she had been killed by a stranger, someone she had allowed into her house but had not known. This could have been a tradesman of some sort or someone posing as an official from one of the utility companies, a meter reader for example. Two, the opposite was true and she had known her killer well, certainly well enough to invite him or her in despite the fact that she was about to go out. This implied confidence on her part were it true. A change of clothes already laid out implied she was about to begin the process of dressing for her appointment at the Worrall house. Quite possibly she was upstairs when someone knocked on the back door. Either way, whoever the visitor was, she had no reservations about inviting them in. Would she have done so had she not felt comfortable in their presence? Third, and perhaps most controversial, there had been more than one killer. When she had answered her door on 18 January it had been to a couple: two people she knew well and quite possibly trusted. There was evidence to support this idea, particularly in view of the fact that she had been attacked with two weapons, a knife and a hammer; certainly these would not have been easily wielded by one attacker. The pattern of wounds could have been inflicted from two different directions at the same time.

When the police team left the Mogano house that night after an exhaustive day exploring all three hypotheses, they were no nearer the truth. All three had merit and the scene they had succeeded in recreating seemed to support each and every one of them. Little of value came from the fingerprint expert; though partial fingerprints were recovered none were likely to prove their worth to the murder team. Then came what appeared initially to be a breakthrough. Police officers carrying out door-to-door enquiries had discovered that on the afternoon of the murder, at a house 180yds away, a bogus electric-meter inspector had talked his way past an unsuspecting housewife. On the premise that he was checking meters and household light switches because of complaints about interference to television sets in the area, she had allowed him into her home. According to her statement he had spent some minutes examining various electrical points around her kitchen, then made sexual advances before she had forced him to leave.

Further police checks across the county then revealed the same man had succeeded in conning his way into another twenty homes. This number increased as more information came in from Birmingham. Sightings of the same man, described as being 25 years old, with thick curly hair, a rosy complexion and wearing a red, plaid shirt, came in from drivers at transport cafés and lorry pull-in sites around Warwickshire. For a while he was a serious suspect, and numerous appeals were made by Coventry police for information as to his whereabouts, but as time passed the notion that he could be Penelope Mogano's killer was not considered credible. As police learned more about their suspect and how he operated, the less they believed in his culpability, and his importance to the investigation began to recede.

At that point the emphasis of the enquiry shifted towards Penelope Mogano's private life. According to the *Coventry Evening Telegraph* the Scotland Yard team began to dig deep into her recent past in an attempt to discover her movements during the afternoons throughout December 1953 and January 1954, up to the time of her death. General enquiries had already revealed that throughout this time, on several afternoons each week, Penelope Mogano had changed her clothes and gone out. Exactly where she went became the puzzle police realised they had to unlock. Again, according to the newspaper, her husband had not been aware of these trips and neither had her close friends, which of course made them all the more mysterious. Unravelling the mystery therefore became a priority, particularly as it became apparent that she had also made key changes to her life in order to facilitate these afternoons out.

In September 1953 it appeared that Mrs Mogano had resigned from the Radford Townswomen's Guild; her reason was exhaustion. According to a spokeswoman from the guild she had told the committee that the number of old-time dancing sessions she and her husband were involved in had proved debilitating, so much so that she needed to rest in the afternoons. At around the same time she had also withdrawn her involvement with foster care, and had returned to the children's home a foster child the family had been caring for. It seemed the more police uncovered the more suspicious they became, but what they needed was a more detailed picture of her daily movements. The only way of achieving that was to ask the neighbours.

As the funeral of Penelope Mogano took place at Canley Crematorium, police took the unprecedented step of handing out 1,500 specially designed questionnaires to people living near the murder site, as well as to homes that would have lined any route she walked out of the district. The questions were simple and effective:

1. Who are regular callers and the reason for them calling? Give day and time.
2. Other callers. Give day and time.
3. Who called on January 18? Time.
4. Do you know Mrs Mogano?
5. Did you see her on January 18?
6. Have you seen her with anyone other than her family?
7. Who calls at 7 Holland Road regularly?
8. Have you seen a car near 7 Holland Road?
9. Are you interested in Old Time Dancing?
10. Are you a member of the Townswomen's Guild?
11. Where were you between 2 p.m. and 5 p.m. on January 18?
12. Any other information?

Once the detail was in police were able to construct a reasonably accurate picture of an average day in the Mogano household. It showed that the daily routines were little different to those of their neighbours. No one saw anything of real significance and the information gathered did not lead to any arrests. However, the fact-finding exercise did appear to uncover one salient fact. Whenever Penelope Mogano left her home after the family lunchtime meal she carried with her a brown paper parcel containing a pair of dancing shoes, the obvious suggestion being that all her afternoon visits were either to a private dancing class or to some sort of private tuition. But despite extensive enquiries throughout the remainder of the year police never discovered the dance teacher.

During late January and early February every tradesman in the area, from milkmen and newspaper delivery boys, to butchers, bakers and insurance salesmen, were all questioned. At around the same time police enquired at all county mental institutions to try and ascertain whether or not any patient had been missing on the day of the murder. But they discovered nothing of relevance in either case. While all this was taking place, the murder squad also seized a quantity of clothing belonging to several men and women. The identity of the owners was never revealed but the clothing was sent to Birmingham's forensic lab to test for bloodstaining. Speculation was that several members of the old-time dancing club were under suspicion, though just how serious those suspicions were was again never disclosed.

Door-to-door enquiries, which had been ongoing since the murder had been discovered, then led police to a telephone kiosk on the corner of Heathcote Street, only 300yds or so from the murder house. A 30-year-old Radford woman told officers that at around 4.25 p.m. on the day Mrs Mogano was killed she had seen a man leave the kiosk with his right hand wrapped in a makeshift bandage. The man – described as being aged 27, 5ft 6in tall, medium build, sallow complexion, pointed chin, sunken cheeks and wearing a black or navy overcoat – had left the phone-box and stood for a number of minutes beside the car in which the woman sat before running off in the general direction of Keresley.

The corner of Heathcote Street today. It does not have a telephone box any more. (Author's Collection)

Once a description of this man had been published by the *Coventry Evening Telegraph*, a second woman came forward to say she believed she had seen the same man thumbing a lift on the Ryton Road. Newspapers across the country then began to carry the story and the same man was traced to Dunstable. From there police were quickly able to establish that he had then obtained a second lift from the driver of a lorry, laden with steel girders, believed to have been heading in the general direction of London. There the trail went cold.

Forensic examination of the telephone kiosk revealed bloodstaining to a telephone directory, which was initially thought to have matched the blood of Penelope Mogano. This was later discounted after it became known a police officer with the same blood group had been cut in a struggle at the same kiosk some weeks earlier. Whoever the man was who had been seen running away it appears he was never found and quite possibly he was never considered a serious suspect.

By February the Scotland Yard detectives appeared to confirm this when, having exhausted the standard lines of enquiry, they issued a statement to the effect that the killer was most probably being shielded by someone. So certain did they appear to be of this that they called a press conference in Coventry and told the gathered reporters they had evolved a three-point theory:

1. That the person shielding the murderer is doing so through fear.
2. That the killer is being shielded because of affection.
3. That this person was a partner in the crime.

It was pure conjecture and suggested that the enquiry was stalling. But what is intriguing is the last point. Up until then police had never openly suggested that the killing could have been carried out by a couple. They had certainly hinted at the idea and included the hypothesis in their initial assessment of the murder scene, though at that time probably not for serious consideration. Yet from the moment Penelope Mogano's body had been discovered with the horrific facial mutilations they must have harboured this belief. The knife attack implied that a woman's hand used the blade. Today it is likely that psychological profiling would perhaps see the killing differently to how it was viewed in 1954. Police investigators more than fifty years on would view the knife wounds as more of a statement than just a frenzied stabbing attack.

Either way, no further leads were forthcoming. Various hitch-hikers were arrested and released, numerous lorry drivers questioned and over 25,000 statements taken, all to no avail. The murder weapon was never found, though three weeks after the murder the Birmingham forensic laboratory was able to say with a degree of certainty that the key murder weapon had been a 2lb round-headed hammer. Police searched gardens and allotments with no success and the case was eventually filed as unsolved.

So who did kill Penelope Mogano? It seems from the evidence available today that police conjecture over the possibility of two killers was a serious one, as was the likelihood that the murderer was a woman. In 1954 the world was a very different place. The vast majority of women did not hold jobs. Instead they ran the household, cleaned, shopped, looked after children and rarely left their immediate neighbourhood except for the occasional bus trip into town. What happened in a street was usually well observed by those who lived closest, and unfamiliar faces were remembered. What makes the Mogano case so baffling is the lack of any of this type of information. She was murdered in broad daylight, and at a time when she was expected to be alone. Both her husband and her son had been home for lunch, which she had prepared. She was anticipated at the Worrall house at 3 p.m.; her change of clothes had already been laid out; she had washed and tidied away the lunchtime crockery, and must have been about to apply her make-up. Is it likely in those circumstances that she would have allowed a tradesman or a salesman into her home? Or is it more likely that she would only have invited someone in she knew? If the latter, then would she have allowed in a man or a woman?

While it would appear that no near neighbour was able to tell police of any visitor that afternoon, that does not necessarily mean they saw none. We often notice and mentally record that which is unusual, but the opposite is true if it is a normal pattern of events. If 18 January 1954 had been a perfectly ordinary day for those living around the Mogano house, then everything they saw while carrying out their usual routines was expected. Traffic at that time was light and car ownership not as it is today, so a strange car would definitely have been noticed. Tradesmen, the odd door-to-door salesman, an occasional gypsy selling lucky heather and women carrying shopping bags or baskets, probably made up an average day. Is it not possible therefore that Penelope Mogano would have felt far more comfortable allowing a woman into her house rather than a man, a woman who perhaps had been shopping? Furthermore, could not a 2lb round-headed hammer be easily carried among that shopping?

Women in 1954 rarely wore trousers and denim was not seen on the streets; they almost always wore dresses and skirts. Whoever killed Mrs Mogano would have been covered in blood; a hammer striking twenty-five times would have splattered the killer's upper torso, impossible to remove while in the house, but some of it would have splashed the hands, face and, in the case of a woman, her legs – all of which could have been washed off easily. Presuming Mrs Mogano knew her killer, then when they entered the house they would have taken off their winter coat and replaced it as they left, so no bloodstaining would have been visible.

Conjecture? Or does it have the ring of truth?

18

THE DEATH OF INNOCENCE

Fillongley, 1955

A t 10 years old Evelyn Patricia Higgins was no different to most of the girls in her class. She was bright, enjoyed most of her time at school, had her favourite teachers, and looked forward to the long summer holidays. She was also very trusting. Despite every caution her mother had taught her, and those the school had constantly re-emphasised, Evelyn trusted all the adults she met – and it was to cost her her life.

At 4 p.m. on 8 June 1955 Evelyn left the Frederick Bird girls' school in Coventry, as she had done every day for the last three years. The day was warm; she had over an hour before her mother finished work so there was no rush to be home and, besides, she had promised to get her hair trimmed after school. Evelyn's trusted hairdresser, Dorothy Hopkins, had a shop on Red Lane, which was only a few hundred yards from the school gates. Leaving her friends behind, Evelyn made it a slow walk. At 5 p.m., with hair cut to her satisfaction, she waved her goodbyes, stepped out of the shop, and vanished.

The entrance to Frederick Bird school. (Author's Collection)

Red Lane today.
(Author's Collection)

Lowther Street today.
(Author's Collection)

Forty minutes later her mother, Joan Higgins, walked in through the back door of their home on Lowther Street. They shared the house with close relative Herbert Mann and his wife, so home was rarely unoccupied for long. If Joan was not home they generally were, which meant that Evelyn always had access regardless of time, so discovering her daughter had not arrived back at the house came as a surprise. She had agreed the visit to the hairdresser and knew that Evelyn, like any other child, was quite capable of dawdling away time, but school had finished over one and a half hours earlier. To Joan's mind that had given her more than ample time to get a haircut and still be home well before half-past five. By 7 p.m. concern had turned to panic. Evelyn was a girl of habit. She rarely stayed outside to play, preferring to watch television, and was always in bed by 7.15 p.m. At that point Joan Higgins probably suspected that if her daughter had not come home then it could only be because something or someone had prevented her.

Police launched an immediate search. Throughout the night they had teams scouring old bomb sites, wasteland, empty houses, and the canal banks and towpaths. By dawn, with the searches having proved fruitless, they were at Evelyn's school in time for 9 a.m. assembly. There, they asked the pupils if anyone could shed light on Evelyn's disappearance. Several said they had seen her en route to Red Lane carrying her distinctive white-edged lunch box at about 4.30 p.m. But then, two girls stepped forward to say they had seen her go past them in a car some forty-five minutes later at the junction of Hartnell Road East and Swan Lane. It was the breakthrough they needed.

Twenty-four hours later they had an eyewitness who identified the car as being a Standard Nine, 1937–8 model, two-door black saloon with a spare wheel sunk in the rear panel. More significantly the registration plate was on the extreme rear offside, not in the centre as was normal, the numbers and letters in a straight line and amateurishly painted. The same witness also gave them a description of the driver: 'Light brown hair, possibly turning grey and brushed back showing the crown of the head, and suggesting that the man was going bald. He was wearing a brownish jacket, no hat, and his general appearance is broad. . . .'

Details were immediately flashed to police forces across the Midlands and the search switched to car parks and parking spaces at factories and workshops.

In 1955 cars were not the common sight they are today. Public transport was good and wages not high enough for many to afford a car of their own, so children developed the habit of carspotting. Books were bought that gave model types and children sought them out and recorded the licence plates in a similar way to how modern-day trainspotters operate, which for the police was an added bonus. For twenty-four hours these children became the focus of police attention. They had already discovered that 9,617 Standard Nine cars had been produced between 1937 and 1938 and had begun the process of tracing every single one of them, but this of course was a mammoth job. What they needed was to be able to narrow the field, and a child with a record of a licence plate that matched any of this number would do exactly that. By Friday 10 June they had found a 13-year-old boy with just such a list.

Police officers arrived at the door of Ernest Charles Harding, a 42-year-old bricklayer, that same evening. At that stage the visit was no more than routine. Harding had been shown as the owner of a Standard Nine identified as being in the relevant area: his car matched the only description they had. It was the right colour, had a hand-written licence plate on the back which was off centre and was almost twenty years old. Nothing about him suggested he was involved in Evelyn's disappearance. Outwardly he appeared calm and relaxed. The police visit seemed to have been expected. Harding had no doubt read earlier press reports identifying the

A Standard Nine of a similar type to that driven by Ernest Harding. (Author's Collection)

*Swan Lane where
Evelyn was last seen.*
(Author's Collection)

Standard Nine car and would have expected police to call as a matter of routine. After a brief discussion he agreed to travel into Coventry the following morning and make a statement and the officers then left.

But Harding had no intention of travelling anywhere. At lunchtime next day, after failing to arrive at the appointed time, his car was discovered some 7 miles outside the city. It was parked off a narrow lane, the accelerator pedal depressed by a stick secured under the driver's seat, and a pipe from the exhaust feeding fumes into the cabin. Harding himself was unconscious on the back seat. His suicide was only averted after officers dragged him from the car and resuscitated him. But the damage had been done, perhaps not physically but certainly circumstantially. In police eyes an attempt to take his life was clear evidence of guilt. No sooner had he recovered his wits than he was hauled into Coventry police station and heavily questioned.

At first he denied any involvement and made two statements in which he insisted he had never been anywhere near Swan Lane on the day of Evelyn's abduction. But then, as if suddenly racked by guilt, he had a change of heart. After an emotional outburst about the shame his failure to die would bring on his family, he admitted murder: 'If I tell you where she is I will not have to go there? I could not bear to see her again.' After asking for pen and paper he then drew a sketch plan of where Evelyn's body could be found.

A police team arrived at Shawbury Wood, Fillongley, late that same day and worked throughout the night in torrential rain. On his hurried sketch Harding had shown the girl's grave just inside the wood but had not been able to be precise as to its exact location. It was dawn on the following morning, Sunday 11 June, that her body was found buried in a shallow grave 8 or 9in below the surface. The body showed signs of having been partially strangled before the throat had been cut.

Later that day Harding was formally charged with murder and appeared in court the following morning where he was remanded in custody. At the inquest held three

The narrow lane that leads to Shawbury Wood. (Author's Collection)

The area of Shawbury Wood where Evelyn's body was eventually discovered. (Author's Collection)

days later at Coventry, Professor James Webster, Home Office pathologist, told the coroner's court that after carrying out his post-mortem examination he was able to confirm his initial findings. Evelyn Higgins, he told a hushed courtroom, had suffered an extremely violent attack, signs of which manifested itself all over her body. She had also been raped. But, he went on, she had most probably been rendered unconscious before her throat had been slashed, the resultant wound being the prime cause of her death. It is probably fair to say that at that point Ernest Harding became the most hated man in Coventry.

The trial opened on 20 July before Mr Justice Lynskey. Defence counsel, Mr Claude Duveen, told the jury at the outset that after all the evidence had been heard he would submit that Harding was insane at the time of the killing. There was little alternative. Harding had already admitted the murder. But what Duveen hoped to be able to show was that at the time of the attack he had suffered a bout of insanity. It was never going to be easy and so it proved.

Detective Inspector Robert Coleman, who had taken Harding's statement admitting the murder, told a hushed court that in his opinion Harding wanted to confess: 'It seemed to me to be a relief to him to get it off his chest.' But the defence counsel, keen to dispel any notion that Harding's statement should be seen as a confession, wanted the inspector to expand on that. They knew that during the interview at Harding's home he had done far more than ease his guilt. During a lengthy cross-examination they pressed the policeman about the notes he had taken with regard to the defendant's past history. What else had he been told during the long interview? The inspector admitted that Harding had offered, as a mitigating reason for his actions, a medical condition that had dogged him all his life. As a baby he had suffered a serious head injury, one for which he still received medical attention and which had left him as an adult suffering indecent impulses. The injury, according to the policeman's notes, had also caused Harding to become moody and irrational and when that happened he had to leave the house. Driving the car around was his antidote.

At that juncture Mr Justice Lynskey, equally keen to dispel Mr Duveen's contention that this was a case of insanity, interjected with a question: 'He volunteered all this information, which might lead to a suggestion that he was insane?' The question, of course, implied that Harding had begun engineering his defence almost as soon as he had admitted his guilt, and if that were so then there could be no doubting his sanity. The inspector confirmed that he had and Mr Duveen finally resumed his seat.

Throughout the remainder of the day there was little solace for either Harding or his defence team as a stream of hostile witnesses took the stand. Professor Webster reiterated his earlier inquest evidence; the investigation team explained how they had been led to Harding's door, and eyewitnesses told of seeing his Standard Nine stop to pick up Evelyn from the street. As the day came to a close, the case for the defence had been seriously compromised and there can be no doubting the despondency all involved must have felt.

On the second day it was decided to put Harding on to the witness stand and let him explain for himself exactly what he had done and why. It was a calculated risk by Claude Duveen but most probably there was little alternative. If insanity was to be proved then it needed to be seen, and where better than in the mind of the man accused of so abhorrent a murder? He began his questioning by asking Harding to explain the nature of his injury and how it affected him. Harding told the court that a second wound inflicted in 1952 had severely aggravated the one he had sustained as a baby. According to his testimony he had been in a fight outside a public house, a fight that had resulted in him being knocked to the ground and had caused a second head injury. This secondary wound had resulted in a total loss of both smell and taste. Furthermore, he had begun to suffer severe headaches and his dizzy spells had worsened significantly.

Duveen: Do you know the expression, blackout?

Harding: I do not know what the expression means, but I had these dizzy
           spells. I would be perhaps standing in the kitchen and everything
           would go and come back again. I told the wife about it and she said
           go to the doctor but I never did.

The defence counsel went on to present more and more information about Harding's
state of health and his apparent ability to lose touch with reality from time to time,
the obvious implication being that he did not remember most of the attack. When he
was satisfied that he had extracted as much detail as was possible he began to
question Harding about the afternoon of 8 June:

I just drove round passing an hour away . . . I was trying to make up my mind
where to go. I turned down Swan Lane and just before I got to the bottom of
Swan Lane I saw this girl walking along by the footpath. . . . At that time I had
no wrong intentions and nothing in my mind. . . I have never picked up a child
or anything before, and whether it was my love for children or what . . . I
thought I would just take her for a drive around. . . . I asked her if she wanted a
drive around and she said yes. When I got through Fillongley I was going to
turn round but I had the old impulse, which drove me on and on. . . . So instead
of turning round I turned left up a lane and pulled up in a gateway. . . .

He went on to describe the attack, how Evelyn had resisted and how he had
placed his hands over her mouth to stop her shouting. But, he claimed, he
remembered nothing of the killing: 'The next thing I can remember she was just lying
there in the back of the car and I noticed blood on her face.' When questioned by the
judge about the knife wounds he denied ever seeing them, and insisted that he had
been so upset at her death that he had never seen the cuts to her neck. When he had
realised that he had killed her, he told the court, he panicked. Then he remembered
the shovel in the boot of his car and decided to drive to a wood he knew well and
bury her. He went on to explain that he had no intention of harming Evelyn when he
offered her the lift in his car and was horrified at what he had done.

Under cross-examination he insisted that his motives had not been sexual when he
had driven the car into Swan Lane. He told the prosecution counsel that when
he killed her in the car he had absolutely no idea he had done so, and even less
that he had used a weapon. When he was asked about how he had come to use a
knife he claimed to have no knowledge of it. He insisted he did not even know he
possessed the knife; furthermore, he had no idea of what he had done with it after
the killing.

As Harding left the stand, Claude Duveen claimed that the reason he had no
recollection was that he had been suffering from epilepsy. To prove the point he
brought a doctor, Arthur Huse, into court. He told the judge that in his opinion
Ernest Harding had suffered a fit before killing the girl, which explained his lack of

memory of the event: 'It was consistent with epilepsy for him to have been in such a condition that he stabbed the little girl without knowing it. . . . Epileptics have what is called automatism – they have a series of movements about which they are ignorant.' The doctor went on to explain his theory in greater detail, defining automatism as a state of mind that in Harding's case would probably have manifested itself after he had carried out the rape. The type of seizure he was describing, he claimed, would have been accelerated by excitement and sexual arousal.

In his closing speech to the jury Claude Duveen insisted that the doctor's evidence be afforded the respect it deserved. The notion of epilepsy, he told the jury, was one not previously realised by either the police or the prosecuting counsel. It was a valid and reasonable explanation of why Harding murdered the girl with a knife, an action of which he had no recollection. According to the defence counsel's speech, when Harding stood in the witness box he had told the truth as he knew it. The fact he had no recall when it came to the actual murder supported the doctor's diagnosis that he had been suffering from the effects of a fit, which had caused the automatism he had so eloquently defined.

Prosecution counsel R.C. Vaughan was having none of it. He told the court that Harding had managed to remember everything he needed to remember, and forgotten only those facts he knew to forget. In other words his memory had been selective. He could recollect stopping his car to pick up the little girl. He could recall where he took her. He could also remember strangling her, but when it came to the knife, which was a clear indicator of intent, he had succeeded in losing his memory. 'Do you', he asked the jury, 'honestly believe that he had no recollection of slashing her throat? It is pretty dreadful to have to admit rape and to having strangled a girl to stop her screaming but that may be a palliation. Cutting her with a knife could not have had any other object but to kill. I invite you to consider whether you believe the defendant when he says that.'

It took ninety minutes for the jury to decide that the medical evidence was flawed and that the prosecution's point had been well made. Harding was found guilty and sentenced to death.

He was executed on Tuesday 9 August by hangman Stephen Wade. A crowd of no more than two-dozen people gathered outside the prison gates to read the notice of execution as it was posted. No voice was raised in protest.

19

MURDEROUS THOUGHTS

Coventry, 1955

James Allan Balloch, 18, had worked at the Midland Bank since he had left school. It was considered a safe and steady job, the kind of work to which many people would have aspired. To work for a bank was to work towards a career. No worrisome future for James. When he was older he would marry, have children, perhaps two, a boy and a girl. It was always good to have one of each. He would slowly climb the slippery slope to success. Eventually he would reach the much vaunted position of bank manager and have his own name plaque on a richly grained oak door that would open into an opulent, modern office all his own. Leastways, that was the plan when he took on the job. But James was far from being manager material. He did not like his work at the bank and harboured secret thoughts of his own. These he told to no one. They were only for himself, but he did write them down.

In these secret writings he was the central character, the hero, the superman. No one controlled his life or built his career. He had set himself free to roam wherever he wished. Sometimes these muses filled his dreams and inhabited his nights. In them his alter ego took control and pushed the normally, shy, retiring James into a dark, hidden corner of his mind. Sometimes, in the mornings, he fancied that this alter ego spoke to him, urged him to break free, escape into a different future, taste something new – commit a murder.

Longfellow Road today.
(Author's Collection)

His mother Winifred probably knew nothing of these secret longings. She was a successful woman. A teacher, she had studied for a degree at Durham University after which she had taught in Sunderland before making the move to Coventry at the end of the war. After her husband's death, which was a difficult time, she and James had settled in Coventry's Longfellow Road, known locally as Poets' Corner, and in 1951 she had taken a post at Churchfield High School. But ambition had not deserted Winifred, and in June 1955 she had won the much coveted role of housemistress at the new Whitley Abbey Comprehensive School, which was due to open its doors in September. So, outwardly at least, she appeared successful both at home and at work. But impressions can be deceptive.

James had been listening carefully to the voices in his head. The murder idea had been growing throughout much of spring 1955, and he had created a whole fictional account of a killing. This he had written down in the form of a short story. Intended for no eyes but his own, it was a gruesome account of a brutal and savage attack on an aged aunt in which he, as the main character, had beaten her to death with a statuette of a horse. So impressed had James been by the imagined act of killing that he had resolved to replicate it in real life, convinced he would be gratified by the experience.

On the morning of 24 July he awoke after a long and detailed dream during which he had been in the post room of the bank. In this dream he was one of a team of

Whitley Abbey school where Winifred Balloch was to take on the role of housemistress in September 1955. (Author's Collection)

bank clerks placing statements into customer-addressed envelopes. Among this team was a young woman, an attractive stranger yet someone he appeared to know well. Throughout the dream he had held on to her hand and known there was an intimacy between the two he had never experienced in his real life, not on a sexual level, more on an emotional one: a kind of familiarity he had often craved but never found; and when he awoke at just after 7.30 a.m., he suffered a very real sense of loss. As he lay in bed trying to hold on to the last vestiges of sleep and recall the face he thought he ought to have known so well, he began to search his mind for a meaning. Of course there was none. The dream had no connection with his real life except in its location and the girl had been pure fantasy. But his sense of well-being as he dreamed had been very real and he wanted to experience it again. Perversely that drew his mind back to the only time he could recall where that sense of needy longing had been satisfied – his story of murder. When he had written the account of the aged aunt's appalling death he had been overwhelmed by a sense of elation. It was time to murder someone for real.

In what to James seemed a rational and logical thought process he debated with himself the pros and cons of carrying out a killing. Finally he accepted that if he was to escape the mundane he must do something remarkable and singular. Murder, he concluded, would satisfy both criteria, purge his body of all unwholesome thoughts and set him free. But then, having accepted the logic of his own argument, he fretted over his mother and how her sensibilities would be severely affected if he did kill someone. The last thing he wanted was for his mother to know her son was a murderer. So, he decided, if he were to prevent her ever finding out about the murder then it must be her that he murdered. Satisfied that this was a fair conclusion he got out of bed, dressed, went downstairs, and from the mantelshelf grabbed the statuette of the horse with which he was so familiar. In an almost mirror image of the fictional account he had so carefully constructed he then went back upstairs. His mother was still sleeping when he entered her bedroom. Raising the statue in his hand he struck her a series of blows to the head. How many is uncertain but when he felt he had done enough to kill her he calmly placed the blood-covered statuette on the dressing table and returned downstairs. There he carried out a second irrational act and called the police: 'Send someone quick. I believe I have done a murder.'

The first policeman on the scene was Sergeant Joseph Smith. He found James sitting outside the house on a wall, his face splattered with blood. All the doors were locked. James told him: 'I have been locked out. I have hit my mother over the head with a horse. She is upstairs.' The sergeant had to force an entry and found Winifred where James had left her, still in bed and despite James's best efforts, still alive. He organised an ambulance but her injuries were so extensive that she died en route to the hospital. James, who never attempted to deny the murder, was taken to Coventry police station and eventually charged with her killing.

At the inquest two days later pathologist James Webster told the coroner's court that Winifred Balloch had sustained a 5in hole in the right side of her head. She had died as a result of shock, a fracture to the skull, haemorrhage and lacerations of the brain. He also told the court that in his expert opinion she had awoken at some point and had sustained defensive wounds to her left hand. The extent of the attack upon her was truly appalling.

James Balloch appeared to show no remorse for what he had done. He made two statements to police. The first, made shortly after his arrest, merely explained why he had killed his mother:

> I did get out of bed and did dress myself. I suppose I must have taken the horse from the mantelpiece in the front room . . . I wasn't feeling particularly nervous or frightened. I had been thinking about a murder and I thought that I wouldn't like my mother to know about it, so it had to be my mother. . . . I have been trying to write it out of me, to write about it to get it out of my system.

The second, which was read to city magistrates when he stood in the dock on 9 August, gave an insight into his state of mind. A rambling document, it is equally intriguing and shows clearly that James was suffering from some form of insanity:

> Murder! I wonder now – yes murder – when have I to do it now? Yes, it will have to be done. I do not believe it though. I really do not believe it. No – I shan't do it. I will go to bed to-night and she will still be living. I will reach 40 and nothing will happen. All the same – no – do not think of that. Repress it and let it come out in a burst. What is the matter with me? I cannot be normal thinking murder like this, but I will not do it – not really. Oh, yes I know that. What's the time? Twenty past, I will get up and then I will see. Now then downstairs, do not make a noise. Be careful, is she asleep? She is not snoring. She might be awake. She might know. If she knows the sooner the better. Where's the horse? I wonder if it is symbolic that horse? What shall I feel I wonder? You won't do it. I am going back – do not run up stairs, not so much noise. One bash and it's all over. I can live in Scotland or Birmingham? What's it matter? I can't hold the thing. What is the best way to do it? Hell I have had no practice. . . .

This is a truly extraordinary document and written by Balloch himself. It reads more like an extract from a novel than a statement made by a man who had murdered his mother.

At his inevitable trial, which opened at Warwick Assizes on 30 November 1955, Balloch pleaded 'not guilty' to murder and these statements formed an integral part of the defence. The second of the two documents was used by his defence barrister, James Ross, to emphasis their assertion that he was clearly insane when he carried out the killing. By way of affirmation he also read extracts from the murder story Balloch had left behind in his bedroom, and told the jury that police had also found a number of books and novels in the house, many of them murder and crime stories.

In the main none of this was contested by the prosecution, though they fell short of accepting Balloch's mental instability as being the cause of his actions. Rather, they contended that a statement detailing guilt was a clear indicator that he did know and understand his own actions regardless of how it had been written. In support of that notion they brought various neighbours to court, most of whom had known James and his mother for a considerable time, to tell the jury that over the years there had been a complete absence of mental frailty. No one, it seemed, had ever noticed that James Balloch had been going quietly mad.

But the medical men won the day. The defence, quite rightly, built their whole case around the testimony of three doctors, all experts in their field of psychiatric medicine and all of whom had been given access to Balloch while he had been held in custody.

Dr Percy Coates, doctor at Birmingham's Winson Green prison, told the jurors that he had examined Balloch both in prison and also as an inmate of nearby All Saints' Mental Hospital:

Balloch had shown no emotional reaction to his position. He had displayed no remorse. On one occasion he had a fit of depression while in hospital. I interviewed him the following day, and during that interview he became rather aggressive and agitated. . . . He said the feelings he had experienced were those he had felt at the time of the offence. . . . He is insane now and certifiable under the Lunacy Act. . . . He is suffering from schizophrenia or primary dementia, it is a disease of the mind.

When challenged on this diagnosis by the prosecution doctor, Coates added that in his opinion when Balloch committed the murder only one part of his mind knew what he was doing, hence the statements he made, but the other part of his mind, perhaps more dominant, did not believe he had done anything wrong.

James O'Reilly, who had helped Dr Coates carry out the assessment at All Saints', concurred, and added that although Balloch did appear to know the nature of the act he had carried out he most certainly did not know it was contrary to the law. This final, and crucial, piece of medical testimony was then endorsed by the defence team's final expert witness, psychiatrist Henry Hauss, who told the court that the evidence in support of mental breakdown was overwhelming.

The jury retired for only ten minutes before returning a verdict of guilty but insane. Mr Justice Streatfield then addressed the court, calling Balloch a Jekyll and Hyde character: 'This is a dreadful tragedy of a mother apparently on good terms with her son, who one morning is peacefully sleeping in her own bed when she is done to death for no apparent reason.' He then sentenced James Balloch to be detained in Broadmoor.

20
A MOMENT OF MADNESS

Coventry, 1957

When 16-year-old David Rooney and his family arrived in Leopold Road, Hillfields, Coventry, it was their sixteenth house move; one for every year of his life. Owing to a sense of insecurity felt by his father, they had been forced almost annually to pack their lives into boxes and move around from town to town until finally they reached Coventry. For David, apart from the obvious upheaval of each and every move, there came the added burden of new schools. By autumn 1957 he had attended six of them, studied under more than thirty different teachers, made and lost numerous friends and never understood the meaning of stability. But throughout it all he managed to remain focused on his education. A sensitive but gifted student, he had won a grammar school scholarship where, through industry and application, he had proven himself to be of higher than average intelligence and gone on to take up an apprenticeship with a local upholsterer.

His father, 46-year-old Thomas, ought to have been immensely proud. But Thomas saw nothing in his son's achievements. A powerfully built man of 16st, he was the dominant force in the house and ruled it with a rod of iron. His will was law and he seemed to see no virtue in his son or his achievements. A physically abusive man, he used his size and his fists to impose his authority on the family. Ignoring David's educational successes he forever referred to him as an immature 13-year-old and belittled his accomplishments at every opportunity.

Leopold Road, Coventry, today. (Author's Collection)

140

But it was against David's mother that Thomas vented much of his anger and most of that anger manifested itself in violence of one form or another. So irrational had Thomas's behaviour become over the years that she had run away from home on no less than six occasions. Each of these attempts to escape his clutches was brought about by an escalation in the violence, and each ended in failure. Among the most recent was an attempt to set up an alternative home in a rented flat in London, but Thomas, as always, succeeded in finding her. On this occasion after threatening violence he smashed all her jewellery and destroyed all her clothes. Left with only a mackintosh to wear she was forced to telephone her sister in Liverpool and ask her to travel to London and collect her. Thomas simply abandoned his wife and returned to Coventry.

Police became involved as the violence increased and eventually he was taken into hospital at Warwick where he was treated for a psychological illness. He stayed there for a few weeks but in the end it made absolutely no difference to how he behaved back at home. Within weeks of being released he had returned to the belligerent, argumentative, bellicose man he had become. None of the anger had dissipated and, despite medical intervention, it was still David's mother who remained his prime target, though David himself was not left unscathed, being dragged downstairs by his hair on at least one occasion and on others finding himself on the receiving end of a tirade of verbal abuse.

So this was the house in which David Rooney spent all of his formative years. Little wonder he began to harbour a sense of resentment and deep-seated anger against his father. He finally snapped on Tuesday 29 October 1957. That night, which in no way differed from any of the preceding nights, Thomas was again haranguing David, this time because he thought his son was making faces at him. His anger steadily grew until he screamed at David to get out of the room. The young lad did as he was told but this time he had had enough. Deciding that it was time to put an end to the ranting of his father, he calmly walked upstairs, picked up the gun he knew was there, loaded it and returned to the kitchen. He gave his father no quarter as he aimed the weapon, fired one shot and killed the man that had made his growing years so miserable. His mother's reaction to the shooting was perhaps understandable: 'Father will get you when he comes round. Go and phone for the ambulance.'

In fact it was to the ambulance driver that David made his first admission of guilt. As he stood watching the medical team in their failed attempt to save Thomas Rooney's life he told the driver that the shot had been no accident: 'He kept nagging me and nagging and so I could stand it no longer and I shot him.' Arrested at the scene he was subsequently charged with murder and after a brief appearance before Coventry Juvenile Court on 1 November he was remanded in prison. On 27 November he stood in the dock at Warwick Assizes before Mr Justice Lloyd Jones and entered a plea of 'not guilty'. Defending counsel, Mr Graham Swanwick, QC, told the court that the killing had been carried out under circumstances which, while perhaps not justified by law, would certainly be understood by any jury; extreme provocation had, he insisted, caused David to take the action he did. The trial itself was short, as was the witness list. There was to be no disputing who shot Thomas Rooney, only why.

Mitigating circumstances were the key as far as the defence team was concerned. With that in mind Detective Inspector James Loughran was brought into the witness box, not just to detail the crime scene but also to tell the court of the events leading to the killing. Under skilful questioning from Mr Swanwick, he detailed the disruption endured by the Rooney family over the past sixteen years. How they had been forced to move home, how David had found it impossible to settle at any school, and of how the young man had witnessed the abuse heaped upon his mother by his father.

As a result of this the defence counsel then requested that the charge of murder be replaced with one of manslaughter. It was a reasonable request given the background to the killing. David had never denied his culpability but, asked the defence, was it murder or an act of desperation? They obviously urged the court to accept the latter and told the judge that they were prepared to enter a guilty plea if he would accept their argument. After a short legal debate Mr Justice Lloyd Jones accepted the defence's contention that there had been no 'malice aforethought', and that the killing, tragic though it was, had been brought about after years of verbal and physical abuse.

At that point the defence then turned to the initial statement David had made to police shortly after his arrest. Mr Swanwick told the court that this was an explanation of the whole thing: 'The incident of October 29 would appear to be insufficient provocation if it were not for all that had gone before.' In a moving address he explained how the family had lived almost in a state of terror and of how Thomas Rooney had imposed his will on them all and dealt cruelly and unkindly with his wife. With the statement in his hand he held it up to the court:

This gives the same picture of an unhappy home and terrible insecurity. Every time his mother came back he saw his father threaten her again. . . . . He was shouting that he was sorry he had married her and had children such as his. . . . This was life with me and my dad. It wasn't only me. He was only on at me every couple of days, but on at mum every night. It was like that every day in the house. . . . He just got you down – arguments and sarcastic remarks. I know I am not too big for my age but my dad was always saying I was only 13 years of age mentally. He was always trying to make me look small.

It was enough to elicit clemency. At the close of the trial David Rooney was sentenced to five years' imprisonment, though the judge, addressing Rooney directly, told him that he had accepted the charge of manslaughter only because he had been subjected over a considerable period to a good deal of provocation.

The act itself was most deliberate. Your father was downstairs and the gun was upstairs. You got the gun, loaded it, brought it down, aimed it at your father and killed him. And you meant to kill him and when spoken to by an ambulance driver you said, he kept nagging and nagging and so I could stand it no longer and I shot him. It seems your father was a very violent man to your

Right: A newspaper headline from 1 November 1957.
(Coventry Evening Telegraph)

Coventry Boy on Murder Charge Again Remanded

SIXTEEN years old David Patrick Rooney, of Leopold Road, Hillfields, Coventry, appeared on remand at Coventry Juvenile Court today on a charge of murdering his father, 46 years old Thomas Rooney, on Tuesday.

He was further remanded in prison for one week.

Rooney first appeared on the charge before Coventry City Magistrates on Wednesday, when the Bench remanded him in custody to today's sitting of the Juvenile Court and also gave permission for his name and address to be published.

Clerk's Query

Today, Det.-Inspector Loughran applied for a further remand for a week in custody. He said: "It is hoped we may possibly be able to go on with the committal proceedings next Friday."

The Clerk, Mr. A. N. Murdoch, asked: "Where is he to go meanwhile?"

Det.-Inspector Loughran replied: "The Chief Constable would ask that the boy be placed somewhere where he is under constant observation."

Mr. J. R. B. Davies, who represented Rooney, told the court: "I have discussed this matter. There is no evidence apart from this particular matter of any unruliness. But I am quite prepared for him to remain where he is."

Mr. F. G. Elliott, presiding, told Rooney: "You will be remanded in custody for a further week. That means you will go back to where you have been for this last couple of days."

The doorway to the cells at Coventry's old police station.
(Author's Collection)

mother and members of your family, but that is no excuse for shooting him, and it would be a pretty sad state of affairs if it was thought that every son when provoked by a violent father was at liberty to take a gun and shoot at him and kill him. . . . There are other safeguards provided in this country. Your mother was able to get a separation order and she need not have gone on living with him. . . . I have to think not only of you, but others who may be tempted to do the same thing. I have to make it perfectly clear to everyone that if that sort of thing is done severe punishment must follow.

There seems little doubt that the judge was somewhat out of touch when it came to violent husbands. Leaving home under such circumstances in 1957 was fraught with difficulty and it would appear that he was unfair in his criticism of David's mother, who had attempted on several occasions to escape her husband's clutches. But at that time there were few avenues open to her that offered safety. Hopefully we are more enlightened today.

21

THE PRICE OF
LODGINGS

Rugby, 1958

Isaiah Dixon, 60, had worked for the Ministry of Transport for just over twelve months. He considered himself lucky to have been selected from among a group of younger, and what he believed to be better-qualified, candidates. With only five and a half years of his working life left when he had sent in his application, he had initially believed his age would have been a barrier, but there was nothing ageist about the ministry. Experience had been their byword since the end of the war and as his stretched back over decades, there had been no discernible reason to bar his selection.

So it was that by winter 1957 he found himself in charge of the office at the Ministry of Aviation's radio-measuring station at Pailton. Wages were not the best in the world but the income was sufficient to allow him to rent a room at a lodging house in Hillmorton Road, Rugby. Still single, despite his best efforts, he had little need of much other than a place to lay his head and a wardrobe to hang up his suit. The lodgings took care of his domestic needs and a variety of nearby pubs ensured he never suffered the life of an insomniac. Unfortunately for Isaiah, though, this tendency to hit the

Hillmorton Road, Rugby.
(Author's Collection)

Market Place, Rugby, c. 1930. Hillmorton Road lay just beyond the square. (Author's Collection)

bottle from time to time also made him vulnerable. When Isaiah drank, the world became a very different place. Inhibitions were lost, stress banished, and unknown acquaintances made into lifelong friends. For the most part these occasions, and there were never very many, had no lasting impact upon his life. But then most of those he knew, or met at a bar, were a part of the night's revelry and therefore generally ended up as inebriated as he did. But in the early spring of 1958 a new lodger arrived at the house on Hillmorton Road; a lodger with a need for cash and an eye for opportunity.

Matthew Kavanagh had travelled over from Ireland to find work some years earlier and for a while had been reasonably successful. Working either as a general labourer or a factory hand he had moved around Warwickshire following the work. As one job ended he had generally succeeded in moving on to another and so had kept the cycle of employment going. But by mid-March 1958 that cycle had come to a shuddering stop after he was laid off from a factory cutting back on labour costs. For Kavanagh it spelled disaster. With no funds set aside to deal with such an eventuality, he was forced to borrow from anybody prepared to lend. But labouring rarely paid well and by April his line of credit had been exhausted. Unable to pay his rent of £3 5s a week he then brokered a deal with his landlady, Mrs McCrum, on the strength of a conversation in a pub. After telling her that he had been offered work, albeit with no definite start date, she agreed to him being in arrears until Monday 14 April. It was the breathing space he needed, and when Isaiah Dixon threw open the door to the lodging house on the Saturday afternoon, two days before his deadline, he saw an end to his problem.

Albert Street, where Isaiah Dixon had been drinking. (Author's Collection)

The Ministry of Aviation man had been in the British Legion on nearby Albert Street since mid-morning. By the time he arrived back at the lodging house at 2.15, he had consumed some sixteen single whiskies. As a result of this indulgence, his cognitive powers were severely impaired, as was his mobility; certainly enough to cause a staircase to take on the appearance of a mountainside, something Kavanagh was astute enough to realise without being prompted. Recognising that Isaiah had begun to struggle the moment his feet met the first step on the stair, he was quick to lend a helping hand. Isaiah was equally quick to accept it. Propped up by his fellow lodger he was then gently pushed, cajoled, and coaxed on to the landing. There Kavanagh took away his key, unlocked his bedroom door, helped the hapless Isaiah into his room, and pushed the door shut behind him. The whole episode was watched by the other lodgers from the hallway below.

The ministry man was too inebriated to care whether the Irishman had stayed in his room or left him alone. The minute his head hit the bed all he wanted to do was sleep. All Kavanagh wanted to do on the other hand was to rob him. For him the solution to his short-term cash-flow problem was lying on the bed in front of him. He had probably made the decision the moment he had stepped forward to help Dixon climb the stairs. But once he had pushed his way into the room, and after Isaiah had fallen on to the bed in a drunken stupor, what had begun as a simple robbery turned into something far more sinister. Whether or not Kavanagh had decided to kill the drunken office manager before he pulled out four £1 notes from the man's trouser pockets or after, is anybody's guess. But at some point he made that decision and turned robbery into murder. Perhaps Isaiah suddenly fought back, which is unlikely, or perhaps the Irishman panicked at the thought of being discovered once the man had sobered up. Either way he determined to remove the risk of discovery forever. Grabbing hold of Dixon's tie, which was still around the man's neck, he slowly strangled him to death. He then left the body where it lay and returned to his own room.

The killing had been quick. Kavanagh had been all too well aware that others in the house had watched the episode on the stairs. If he was to feign innocence when the body was eventually discovered he knew he had no time to linger. The longer he spent in Dixon's room the more likely accusing fingers would be pointed his way. So, of necessity, both the murder and the robbery were carried out within minutes of Isaiah stumbling towards his bed. Kavanagh then spent much of the afternoon sleeping.

Isaiah Dixon was not expected to surface until breakfast the next day. Those who had witnessed his drunken state would have calculated the remainder of Saturday as being a reasonable recovery period and they would have been quick to tell others. So, with time on his side, Kavanagh knew he was safe from immediate censure and delation. Misgivings over Isaiah's well-being would not be raised until Sunday, a non working day for everyone at the house. That was when the various lodgers would gather and Isaiah's drinking binge would be top of their agenda. So, there was unlikely to be any discovery of the body until Sunday lunchtime at the earliest. But what was he to do then? Kavanagh's sleep was a troubled one.

Later that evening he walked into Coventry and, over the course of two or three hours, spent three of the four £1 notes he had stolen in various shops and pubs. There was no doubt he had a lot to think about, not least how he was to explain away his involvement in the ministry man's death. The last man seen with the victim, robbery an obvious motive, and the body found in a locked room – these were three key facts that probably caused him a deal of concern. But it was this last of the three that he probably saw as his greatest challenge and the one he realised would be his eventual undoing. The door into Isaiah's room was secured by a Yale lock; in his panic to escape the murder scene he had dropped the Yale behind him when he left but not taken the keys. The killing could, therefore, only have been committed by someone who made a forced entry.

At 10.30 that night, after exhausting all his options, he walked into Millicent's Café on Far Gosford Street, Coventry, and told the owner, a Mr Steele, that he had

Two views of Far Gosford Street today. Millicent's Café was on the left near to the roadworks.
(Author's Collection)

147

killed a man. Furthermore, he went on to explain exactly how and why. Kavanagh, it appeared, had decided to abandon subterfuge and tell the truth, though the veracity of his eventual statement was somewhat less than genuine. Candour was not a characteristic Kavanagh was familiar with. When police first questioned him at the café he made no mention of robbery being his motive for the killing. Instead he attempted to convince the investigating officers that the death had been both unintentional and accidental.

According to his version of events, it had been Isaiah Dixon's drunken state that had caused his own death. He, Kavanagh, was simply an innocent victim. He told police that when he had stepped forward to offer help to his fellow lodger he had not realised just how intoxicated he had been. So bad was he, claimed Kavanagh, that when the two of them eventually managed to stumble into the bedroom, Isaiah had fallen forward on to the bed. The momentum of that fall had dragged the Irishman down on top of him and as a consequence Isaiah had suffocated. It was plausible but unfortunately for him not borne out by the facts.

When Detective Inspector Tavinor opened Isaiah's room door with a master key some two hours later, he found his body on the bed with a black tie pulled tight around the neck. Nothing in the room had been disturbed. The bed had not been disarranged, drawers were open but nothing appeared to have been removed. The only item missing was money. None was found either on his body, inside any of his clothes, within the wardrobe, or hidden anywhere in the room. To Tavinor it seemed obvious that Kavanagh had lied and that far from investigating an accidental death, he was in the middle of a murder scene. Local doctor Robert Hearn dispelled any lingering doubts an hour or so later when he confirmed that death had been due to strangulation. He also stated that marks around the neck were consistent with the black tie being used to effect that strangulation. At that point, as far as the inspector was concerned, it was an open and shut case. Kavanagh had almost certainly murdered him and the lack of money in the room indicated robbery as the motive.

Questioning the lodgers, despite the early hour, quickly established that the dead man had been in full-time employment, paid a wage on the Friday afternoon, was up to date with his rent and had no known creditors. This was a man who paid his way through life, saved a little when he could, enjoyed a drink from time to time but generally kept himself to himself. The Irishman on the other hand appeared to have been a complete antithesis to all this. As the lodgers gave their statements, and almost as an adjunct to the facts they offered up about the dead man, they confirmed what Tavinor had begun to suspect, namely that Kavanagh was desperately short of cash. Most had been approached to lend him money. Most knew he had not worked for a few weeks. If any doubts remained after all the statements had been collected in they were more about why, rather than how. Tavinor must have been convinced at that point that he had gathered enough evidence, albeit circumstantial, to challenge the Irishman's version of events. As far as the police investigation team went, there was little doubt in everyone's mind when they left Hillmorton Road that Kavanagh was a murderer. He was not about to disappoint.

When eventually confronted with police suspicions later that same morning at Rugby police station, he immediately confessed. It seemed to come as a relief when he finally admitted that he had killed the ministry man in order to rob him. No money to call his own and a mounting debt were the mitigating factors. Isaiah, he told the police inspector, had simply been in the wrong place at the wrong time. Vulnerable through drink he had presented an unexpected, and unlooked for, opportunity. According to his amended version of events, murder had not been his intention and he never explained how or why he did it. But he did admit to the theft of four £1 notes and some silver coins, which was all he found in the man's room. When he had stepped forward to help Isaiah up the stairs he, too, he told Tavinor, had consumed a fair amount of alcohol. This he thought had impaired his judgement and caused him to act out of character or else he would never have carried out the attack.

Kavanagh was formally charged with murder, and two days later remanded to prison to await his trial. While on remand, perhaps troubled by his conscience, he dictated a letter to his mother in Ireland. The letter was in essence a confession. It may have helped him sleep, but it did nothing to help him in court:

> I was half drunk and broke in my digs at Rugby when another lodger came in also half drunk. I thought I would be able to touch him for £1 or 10s. I got him to the door of his room where he had some difficulty in finding his keys. I went to assist him. . . . All this time he was making a fuss of me. His arms were over my shoulders and he kept rubbing his face up against mine. I did not know what I was doing and I strangled him with his neck-tie. I went through his pockets and took out £4 in notes and some silver.

This was a document that effectively damaged his defence irrevocably – murder in the course of robbery was a capital offence and if a jury agreed, he would go to the gallows. Whether or not he had been made aware of such a fact is not known.

On 2 July 1958 Matthew Kavanagh, in a brown suit and wearing horn-rimmed spectacles, took his place in the dock at Warwick Assize Court and pleaded 'not guilty'. He had had nearly three months to consider his situation and how best to defend himself. The path chosen by his defence counsel, Mr J.A. Grieves, was that chosen by Kavanagh back in April when he stood in Millicent's Café. There was no murder, just an accident. In light of his own confession that was not going to be easy to prove.

As counsel for the Crown rose to address the court at the opening of the trial they must have felt – much as perhaps police inspector Tavinor had after walking into Isaiah Dixon's room – that the case was a foregone conclusion. The evidence against Kavanagh appeared to be overwhelming. Everything the police had uncovered with regard to the circumstances surrounding the killing indicated the Irishman's guilt. Even statements he had made and the damning letter to his own mother supported the hypothesis that his guilt was unquestionable. But it was mainly conjecture.

No one had witnessed Kavanagh committing the murder. No one had entered Dixon's bedroom on any of the days leading up to his death who could corroborate the belief that he had stored money away. Nor could anyone with any degree of certainty confirm that the dead man had any money on his person when Kavanagh half-carried him into that room. In fact there was absolutely no evidence available that was not insurmountable and Kavanagh's defence team knew it. The case was going to prove far harder to win than anyone had imagined at the outset.

Nevertheless, prosecuting counsel, Mr R.K. Brownal, gave no outward signs of his case being anything other than certain when he began his opening address. He also left no doubt in any juror's mind of exactly what they were being asked to consider: 'If murder is committed in the cause of furtherance of theft it is what the law describes as capital murder and if the charge is proved the sentence is death.' There was no ambiguity in his choice of words. When he sat down and the trial began proper, there could be no doubt in those twelve jurors' minds that Matthew Kavanagh was about to begin a fight for life.

Throughout the first day the jury were introduced to a number of witnesses, each of whom laid the foundation of the police case. Enoch Pincus and Daniel Callaghan, both lodgers at the house on Hillmorton Road, described in detail the events of Saturday 12 April: how they had stood at the bottom of the stairs and watched Kavanagh help the drunken office manager into his room. Pincus also told the court that he knew Kavanagh to be unemployed and short of money. That evidence was further supplemented by former lodger, William Quirk, who told how he had met with the Irishman during the morning of that same Saturday in Rugby. Kavanagh had no money and the two men had discussed his worsening financial situation. Detective Inspector Tavinor described the murder scene, how Kavanagh had reacted to initial questioning, how he had at first lied, then amended his statement, and how when searched he had been found in possession of a £1 note and some loose change.

Then, almost as a *coup de grâce*, prosecution counsel brought Elsie Manners into court. In many ways it was her albeit brief evidence that caused the greatest amount of concern to the defence team. She told a hushed courtroom how Matthew Kavanagh had walked into her husband's clothier's shop late that same day and paid £1 for a new shirt, the obvious implication being that if at the start of the day he had no money in his pocket, how did he manage to buy the shirt and still end the day with a surplus? It could only have happened if he had robbed Isaiah Dixon.

On the second day, with testimony from the prosecution witnesses exhausted, the court was given over to the defence team. This was an opportunity for them to place before Mr Justice Streatfield a different version of events, a version that would perhaps save Kavanagh from the noose. But they called no witnesses. Instead they accepted that Kavanagh had committed robbery, but that the death following that robbery had been unintentional.

Isaiah Dixon, contested Mr Grieves, had died as a result of vagal inhibition; a sudden muscle reflex or spasm that could have stopped his heart and been caused by an accidental blow to the solar plexus. Such an event meant Kavanagh had not been responsible for the death at Hillmorton Road. He went on to argue in support of that notion that both men had drunk a large amount of alcohol, but Isaiah had consumed the most. In fact his consumption of some sixteen shots of spirit had made him as unpredictable as only a drunken man could be. He would not have known too much about his surroundings. He would also not have been too aware of exactly who was helping him to climb the stairs. Once inside his room, contested the defence counsel, he would most probably have become extremely unsteady and his movements somewhat erratic. By that time Kavanagh had half-carried him a fair distance; a distance that in the cold light of a sober day may not have appeared too great, but a troublesome one when encumbered with a writhing, unstable, heavy weight on his back. Addressing the jury, he asked them to consider what this would have meant to Matthew Kavanagh. How, when he managed to get into Dixon's room he would probably not have been able to control the man's weight when he tumbled forward towards the bed. That in all probability had caused Dixon to fall on his face, which in turn had precipitated the deadly spasm, and then just as Kavanagh had first insisted when stood in the Coventry café, had resulted in suffocation.

There was serious merit to the argument, particularly in light of the inebriated state of both men; furthermore, as Mr Grieves argued so eloquently, no irrefutable evidence existed of murder:

> The prosecution is inviting you [the jury] to believe that he entered the bedroom with the intention of murdering Dixon for his money. . . . Use common sense. You cannot leave out of account the state Dixon was in. . . . We have medical evidence Dixon must have consumed at a minimum sixteen single measures of spirits. If you are going to steal the money of a man in that condition do you need to murder him? You have got to use a sense of proportion. . . . Was it murder in the course of theft or in the furtherance of theft? There were only suggestions that it was in the furtherance of theft. If the Crown cannot make up its mind, how can you be expected to?

It was a powerful defence and certainly one that demanded close attention, but not one shared by either the prosecution or the judge. The Crown were quick to point out the flaws in Mr Grieves's contention that the defendant could not have committed murder; most serious of which being Kavanagh's own confession to the killing: 'I did not know what I was doing and I strangled him with his neck-tie. I went through his pockets and took out £4 in notes and some silver.' That alone, they contested, was enough to show his guilt. Had he been innocent would he have made such an admission and would he have had cash in his pocket at the end of the day? There seems little doubt the judge agreed with that view.

In his summing up, he told the jury there was no evidence that Kavanagh had acted under the sting of provocation, sexual or otherwise, which could have amounted to a manslaughter verdict. There was also no evidence that he was so drunk as to be incapable of forming an intention to kill. The only choice, he pointed out, was between being not guilty of capital murder or guilty of murder. Meticulously, he then covered all the salient points of the case, outlining both defence and prosecution arguments and the veracity behind those arguments. When he came to the defence's contention that it had been a type of medical phenomena that had caused the death of Isaiah Dixon he reaffirmed the examining doctor's findings. Death had been caused by strangulation and the black tie around the neck had done the necessary damage.

For the retiring jury there was therefore no room to manoeuvre and after just forty minutes they returned the expected verdict of capital murder. Donning the black cap Mr Justice Streatfield then passed the sentence of death on Kavanagh. Six days later an appeal was lodged with the Home Office but summarily dismissed and Matthew Kavanagh was executed at Birmingham on Tuesday 12 August. The hangman was Harry Allen.

Some time after his trial it transpired that Matthew Kavanagh had in fact been in court one year earlier on a similar charge. In June 1957 he was arrested after he had made a phone call to police in Birmingham and admitted he had been involved in the death of a woman named Evelyn Ulla. Her body was eventually found near to the Wheatsheaf Hotel in Sheldon, on the outskirts of the city. According to Kavanagh's statement at the time, the two of them had been to the cinema and later, several pubs. While walking home she had complained of the cold. He claimed he had then taken hold of her scarf to pull it tighter and she had suddenly collapsed, dead, at his feet. He was subsequently charged with her murder but when he made an initial appearance in the Birmingham Magistrates Court the charge was reduced to one of manslaughter. In the court's opinion, post-mortem evidence had lacked the necessary detail to ensure a conviction. Enough doubts had been raised to prosecute murder with any real conviction. At his trial later that same year, these same doubts resurfaced a second time. After hearing some of the evidence, Mr Justice Lynskey eventually stopped the proceedings and directed the jury to acquit Kavanagh on the grounds that insufficient evidence existed to bring the case to a fair conclusion. It was suggested at the time that Evelyn may well have died as a result of vagal inhibition. Kavanagh walked from the court a free man and moved to Rugby shortly afterwards.

Whether or not Kavanagh murdered Evelyn Ulla will now never be proven. What is certainly strange is that the same defence used in that Birmingham trial figured once more in what appears to have been a very similar death. Therefore it has to be a distinct possibility that Matthew Kavanagh was a double murderer. In 1958 his rare defence strategy failed, not because the theory behind such a defence was flawed, but because he had used a neck-tie that had left behind distinct and tell-tale signs of violence. Vagal inhibition leaves almost no external trace on a body. Perhaps it could be argued that justice finally prevailed.

INDEX